POTPIES

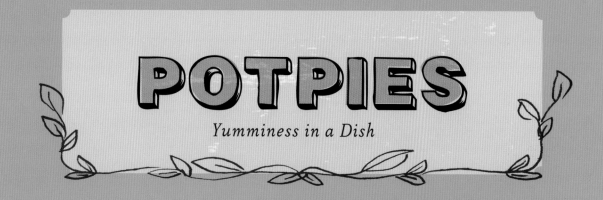

POTPIES

Yumminess in a Dish

By **ELINOR KLIVANS**   Photographs by **SCOTT PETERSON**

CHRONICLE BOOKS

SAN FRANCISCO

Library of Congress Cataloging-in-
Publication Data available.

ISBN-10: 0-8118-5161-3
ISBN-13: 978-0-8118-5161-9

Manufactured in China.

Designed by Vivien Sung
Prop styling by Emma Star Jensen
Food styling by Andrea Lucich
Typesetting by Janis Reed

Distributed in Canada by
Raincoast Books
9050 Shaughnessy Street
Vancouver, British Columbia V6P 6E5

10 9 8 7 6 5 4 3 2 1

Chronicle Books LLC
680 Second Street
San Francisco, California 94107

www.chroniclebooks.com

DEDICATION

As always, for my family—Jeffrey, Laura, Michael, Charlie,
Peter, Kate, Madison, Max, and Sadie

ACKNOWLEDGMENTS

Judith Weber, my agent, who makes my books happen.

Bill LeBlond, my editor, who gives me such great ideas to work on.

Amy Treadwell, assistant editor, who managed every detail of this book from the speck of an idea to its "hot and bubbling" finish.

Many thanks to Doug Ogan, Evan Hulka, Brett MacFadden, Steve Kim, copy editor Carolyn Miller, and the brilliant publishing team at Chronicle Books.

Scott Peterson, whose photographs make you want to dig in, and his team—food stylist Andrea Lucich, prop stylist Emma Star Jensen, and photo assistant Tiffany Fosnight.

My husband, Jeff, who truly enjoyed every single potpie.

My daughter, Laura, who cheers me on, tests recipe, and proofreads, and my son-in-law, Michael, who is such a good listener.

My son, Peter, who proofread, cooked, and always found time to talk about food and potpies; and my daughter-in-law, Kate, who was organized enough to test recipes in the midst of their ever-growing family and new jobs.

My mom and dad, who taught me the value of a family eating and enjoying food together.

Thank you to the potpie testers who tested so many recipes: Heather Barger, Laura Klivans, Peter Klivans, Melissa McDaniel, Dawn Ryan, Louise Shames, Kate Steinheimer, Dana Strickland, and Laura Williams.

A big thank-you to my circle of supporters and encouragers: Melanie Barnard, Flo Braker, Sue Chase, Susan Dunning, Natalie and Harvey Dworken, Carole and Woody Emanuel, Mutzi Frankel, Karen and Michael Good, Kat and Howard Grossman, Helen and Reg Hall, Carolyn and Ted Hoffman, Pam Jensen and Stephen Ross, Kristine Kidd, Alice and Norman Klivans, Dad Klivans, Susan Lasky, Robert Laurence, Rosie and Larry Levitan, Gordon Paine, Joan and Graham Phaup, Janet and Alan Roberts, Jack and Susan Rockefeller, Louise and Erv Shames, Barbara and Max Steinheimer, Kathy Stiefel, Gail Venuto, Elaine and Wil Wolfson, and Jeffrey Young.

CONTENTS

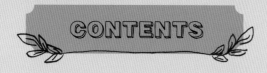

INTRODUCTION

A surprising thing happened the morning after I finished testing the potpies for this book. My husband, Jeff, asked for a potpie—any potpie—for dinner. After a year of eating several hundred potpies, my husband wanted even more. Proof positive that, as my friend Will Easton said with a sigh when he heard about this book, "There is nothing like a potpie."

Potpies were originally pies cooked in a pot over an open-hearth fire. Their top crust sealed in their juices and kept them moist during cooking. Nowadays, potpies bake evenly and quickly in the oven and can have a variety of toppings and fillings. They do not have a bottom crust that could become soggy, and typical potpie baking dishes hold generous quantities of filling. Some potpies are finished with pastry crusts, crumb toppings, tortillas, or phyllo pastry that adds a crisp-all-the-way-through topping. Some use biscuits, corn bread, or sliced potatoes for toppings that are crisp on the outside and soft inside. The classic choice for a creamy, soft topping is mashed potatoes. Although fillings often include a gravy or sauce, others can simply be moist. Examples of these are the ground meat and onion filling of an empanada potpie (page 51) or the filling for a spinach, ricotta, and Parmesan potpie (page 125).

Potpies are easy to prepare and will fit into any occasion. They use readily available ingredients, often make a one-dish meal, and can serve one person or a crowd. Most can be put together at your leisure and baked later in the day, and many can even be frozen, ready and waiting to be defrosted and popped in the oven to bake.

The more I baked them, the more I understood the lure of potpies. They're all about comfort and satisfaction—all the way down to the bottom of the potpie dish.

FILLING the POTPIE

ALL ABOUT POTPIE FILLINGS & TOPPINGS

Potpie fillings come in unlimited combinations, but their common thread is that they use simple cooking methods. Potpie techniques run the gamut from simply stirring shrimp with seasonings and butter for a shrimp scampi filling to slow-cooking a chicken in a rich red wine sauce.

Potpie fillings have some common characteristics. The ingredients should be bite-size. Any ground meat, meat, or chicken should be cooked thoroughly before being baked with the topping. Meat that is not ground, such as the steak in a Swiss steak potpie, is also cooked before it is baked as a potpie. The purpose of the final baking in the oven is to heat the filling and bake the topping. An exception is seafood or fish that cook quickly. These can be baked along with their topping. Fillings can include either a simple sauce or gravy or a moist filling, such as that for a ground beef and onion empanada. The baking container should be large enough to leave space between the filling and topping so that the filling does not bubble up through the topping and saturate it.

A method often used for cooking potpie fillings is to soften or brown the vegetables or meat in a small quantity of oil or butter. Then liquid is added to simmer the ingredients to the level of doneness. The cooked filling should cool (often for about 15 minutes) before adding a topping. A crust could soften and melt if put on top of a steaming hot filling.

Potpies have toppings (often crust, but not always), but no bottom crusts. A nice bonus is that there is no possibility of a soggy bottom crust. The topping choices are as varied as those of the fillings. Toppings include crusts of many kinds: phyllo pastry, mashed potatoes, sliced potatoes, biscuits, dumplings, a quick soda bread, tortillas, nut crumbles, or breadcrumb crusts. Crusts can be made from scratch, or a good quality store-bought one can be used. Toppings and fillings can be mixed and matched. I have given some crust choices in the recipes, but if your taste runs to mashed potatoes rather than a pastry crust, that is fine. There are no "potpie police" in this pie world, and personal taste is a good guide.

PEELING TOMATOES AND POTATOES EASILY
Tomatoes Have ready a large bowl filled with water and ice cubes. Half-fill a medium or large saucepan with water and bring it to a boil. Use a slotted spoon to gently drop the tomatoes into the water. Leave for 30 seconds and use the spoon to remove the tomatoes to the ice water. As soon as they are cool enough to handle, remove the tomatoes from the cold water, and slip off and discard the skins. The tomatoes are ready to use.

When it is not tomato season, peeled canned tomatoes make a good tomato choice.

Potatoes Put the potatoes in a medium or large saucepan (depending on the quantity of potatoes) and add water to cover by at least 1 inch. Bring the water to a boil. Loosely cover the pot and cook the potatoes for 20 minutes. The outside (about 1/2 inch deep) will be soft and the inside still firm. If the potatoes need to cook completely, continue cooking them until they test tender with a fork, about 20 additional minutes depending on the size of the potatoes. Put a colander in the sink and carefully pour the potatoes into it, draining off the water. Run cold water over the potatoes until they are cool enough to handle. Use a small knife to help slip the skins off the potatoes.

GENTLE BOILING AND SIMMERING Many potpie fillings cook at a gentle boil or a simmer before they bake. A gentle boil has a few large bubbles if you are not stirring it. Simmering liquid has tiny bubbles, and most of them will be around the edge of the pan.

POTPIE INGREDIENTS

Check your recipe ingredient list to see what you need to buy. Pantry ingredients should also be checked for freshness and replaced if necessary. One organized trip to the market saves a lot of time. In all cases, look for fresh ingredients and buy the best quality you can find.

Butter, shortening, and oils Do not use reduced-fat butter. It has water added and reacts differently in a recipe than butter does. I use unsalted butter and add salt to the dish as needed. To keep it fresh, store unsalted butter in the freezer. For vegetable shortening, I use Crisco and buy it in the easy-to-measure stick form. When a recipe calls for vegetable oil, I use corn or canola oil, and for olive oil I choose extra-virgin olive oil from the first pressing of olives. Taste or smell all oils to check that they have a fresh smell and taste and have not turned rancid.

Eggs Large eggs are used for the recipes in this book.

Flour and cornmeal I use unbleached all-purpose flour. Store cornmeal in the refrigerator to keep it fresh.

Herbs and spices Store dried herbs or spices tightly covered in a cool, dark place and check them for freshness. Storage times and conditions vary for different spices; a simple solution is the taste test. If the herb or spice is stale, it will have little or no taste. When substituting dried herbs for fresh, a general rule is that 1 teaspoon of crushed dried herbs is equal to 1 tablespoon of chopped fresh herbs.

Fresh herbs are readily available in supermarkets and are easily grown in pots on a sunny windowsill. Most fresh herbs with stems can be stored in a jar of water at room temperature for about 1 week. Change the water every day. Cut herbs can be wrapped in paper towels, placed in plastic, and stored in the refrigerator. Wash them just before using them. The storage times for fresh herbs vary, and the best way to tell if an herb is in good condition is to look at it and smell it. Fresh herbs look green, with no black or brown spots, and smell of the herb. Fresh basil, used often in my recipes, has a fairly short storage life. The best way to have it on hand is to keep a pot growing indoors or outside. Otherwise, try to buy fresh basil just before you are going to use it. Keeping it dry, wrapped in a paper towel and a plastic bag, and refrigerating it yields the longest storage time, 2 to 3 days. Fresh thyme has a storage time of as long as a month if kept dry, wrapped in plastic, and refrigerated.

Lemon and orange zest The zest is the outside, colored part of the rind of lemons and oranges. Grate only the colored part; the white pith under the zest is bitter. Wash and dry the fruit before grating it. A Microplane grater, patterned after a woodworker's rasp, is the best tool for grating citrus zest.

Meat, fish, and poultry Lean meats, very fresh fish, and fresh chickens are obviously best. For ground beef, buy at least 85 percent lean. Look for fish that is bright-eyed (if whole) and shiny. Fish should have a pleasant odor and not smell "fishy." Buy from a reliable fish market. It is preferable to use all meat, fish, and poultry the day that it is purchased and certainly within twenty-four hours.

Although it is unlikely that they are contaminated, it is safest to treat all fresh meat, fish, poultry, and eggs with care. I prepare these foods on a clean dish and then wash the dish and any utensils that have come in contact with them in the dishwasher or very hot soapy water. Clean any cutting surfaces that come in contact with the meat, fish, poultry, or eggs with a sanitizing solution of 1 tablespoon of bleach mixed with 4 cups of water. Finally, wash your hands with soap frequently, and for at least 20 seconds for each washing. Remember, even if the chance of contamination is slim, it only takes seconds to keep food and preparation areas clean and free of bacteria.

Milk and cream I have noted in the recipes whether the recipe needs milk with a particular fat content. Buttermilk is low-fat or fat-free milk that has been cultured with bacteria. It has a thick texture and slightly sour taste. I use fat-free buttermilk in my recipes. I use heavy whipping cream (36 to 40 percent butterfat) when recipes call for cream.

Nuts The new crop of nuts appears in supermarkets from September to December, and this is a good time to buy a year's supply. Store them in the freezer in a tightly sealed heavy-duty freezer bag or plastic freezer container for up to 1 year or in the refrigerator for up to 1 month.

Chopping nuts with a large, sharp knife gives good control over the size of the chopped nut. Finely chopped nuts should be about 1/8 inch in size, and coarsely chopped nuts between 1/4 inch

and 3/8 inch in size. For ground nuts, use a food processor. Processing the nuts with some of the sugar or flour from the recipe allows the nuts to become finely ground without forming a paste.

To toast nuts, spread them out in a single layer on a baking sheet and bake them in an oven preheated to 325°F. Bake blanched sliced or slivered almonds for about 12 minutes, or until they become golden, and blanched whole almonds for about 15 minutes, or until they become golden. Just before the nuts are ready, you will smell a pleasant aroma of toasting nuts.

Salt and pepper I use kosher salt, which is free of preservatives and has a clear, fresh taste. Ground black pepper becomes dry and flavorless quickly, so I keep a pepper grinder filled with whole peppercorns and grind pepper as I need it.

Vegetables Take a good look at vegetables before buying them. Broccoli and carrots should be firm and crisp. Onions should be firm and free of mold. Choose young, firm eggplants and zucchini. Sweet peppers and tomatoes should have no soft spots. Fresh garlic should not have green stems in the center of the cloves; if yours does, remove it before using. Coarsely chopped vegetables are about 1/4 inch in size. Finely chopped vegetables are about 1/8 inch in size.

COOKED CHICKEN & CHICKEN BROTH

1 pound chicken breasts, thighs, or a combination

1 onion, quartered

1 carrot, peeled

4 sprigs fresh parsley

3 black peppercorns

1 bay leaf

Cooking chicken and making chicken broth is a two-for-one process. They can be cooked at the same time in one pot. The idea is to add seasonings to the water when cooking chicken for a potpie and have the cooking liquid become the broth for the potpie. Both are used often for these potpies.

NOTE: Chicken on the bone should be used to add a rich flavor to the broth. But it is handy to know that 1 pound of boneless chicken yields about 4 cups of cooked chicken. To avoid a possible chlorine taste in broth, make it with spring or filtered water.

Combine the chicken, onion, carrot, parsley, peppercorns, and bay leaf in a large saucepan with water to cover by about 2 inches. Cover loosely and bring to a gentle boil (a few bubbles). Use a spoon to skim off and discard any foamy surface residue. Cook until the chicken is opaque throughout, about 30 minutes. Use tongs to remove the chicken to a plate. Remove and discard any skin. As soon as it is cool enough to handle, pull the meat off the bones. Cut the chicken into the size needed for the recipe and refrigerate for up to overnight, if not using immediately.

Return the bones to the broth. Continue cooking the broth, uncovered, for at least another 30 minutes. Taste the broth (after cooling it on the spoon), and if it has a good chicken flavor, strain the broth into a large bowl. Discard the bones and seasonings. (Any salt and pepper will be added when the broth is added to a filling.) The broth is ready to use or it can be covered and refrigerated for up to 2 days. Or, the broth can be sealed in freezer containers and frozen for up to 1 month.

Choices: Substitute 2 pounds of beef or veal bones and a 4-ounce piece of beef or veal for the chicken. Roast the bones and meat for about 45 minutes at 375°F, or until they brown. Cook the beef and bones with water and the same seasonings, plus a tomato, as described above for the chicken. Taste the broth after 1 hour to see if it has a good meat flavor. The meat will not be used in the potpie recipes, but it can be eaten, if desired.

EQUIPMENT FOR MAKING & CONTAINERS FOR BAKING POTPIES

Equipment for making potpies is basic. Several sizes of pots and pans, an assortment of common utensils, and baking dishes are all that is needed.

Baking dishes Baking containers can dress up or dress down a potpie. Any ovenproof baking dish can be used for potpies. Each recipe gives a measurement or capacity requirement so that the container will be large enough to hold filling and topping. Baking containers that I use often include a shallow white round baking dish that is 9 inches in diameter and 2 inches deep; three soufflé dishes that hold 4, 6, and 8 cups respectively; a 9-inch-diameter Pyrex glass pie dish that is 2 inches deep; and ovenproof soup bowls with a 2-cup capacity.

When recipes call for a container size such as 8 cups, a slightly larger container (2½ quarts) is fine. Rectangular and oval shapes make a nice change. If in doubt about the capacity of a baking container, use a measuring cup to fill the container with water and count the number of cups the container holds.

I try to fit the color of the baking dish to the kind of potpie. Bright vegetable potpies look nice in white containers, while homey potpies such as Chilaquiles Potpie (page 26) or Black Bean Chili Potpie with Onion and Pepper Corn Bread Topping (page 122) look nice in a colorful or dark rustic container.

Ovens Most potpies are baked in the oven. You will notice that there is a visual test and an approximate baking time for baking each potpie. Ovens vary in how they bake, so keeping a close eye on a potpie during baking is important. It is a good idea to use an oven thermometer to make sure the oven temperature is accurate. A clue that there might be a problem with the calibration of your oven is when your crusts suddenly begin burning or underbaking during a normal baking time.

Pots and pans Medium-size skillets and sauté pans are about 8 inches in diameter while large ones are 12 inches in diameter. Choose saucepans with stainless-steel or nonstick interiors, which will not react with acidic foods. Unlined aluminum, unlined copper, and cast-iron pans can react with such acidic foods as buttermilk or tomatoes. A small saucepan holds 4 cups, a medium saucepan 8 cups, and a large saucepan 3 or 4 quarts. A large pot for boiling pasta or a large quantity of filling should hold at least 5 quarts.

SERVING, STORING, MAKING AHEAD, TRANSPORTING & FREEZING POTPIES

Serving Dishing up potpies usually means simply using a large spoon to scoop out crust and filling or a sharp knife to cut portions. They lend themselves to a help-yourself serving style. Potpies are usually served hot. The topping insulates the filling, so that a potpie in its baking container will often remain hot throughout a meal.

Storing and making ahead Many potpie fillings can be prepared ahead, covered, and refrigerated overnight. Some of the recipes note when the potpie can be completely assembled, with its topping added early in the day or the day before baking. Most leftover potpies can be reheated the next day. Cover the potpie tightly with aluminum foil and reheat it in a preheated 350°F oven. The time will depend on the size and type of potpie.

Transporting The best potpies to transport are ones that do not have a lot of liquid filling that can slosh around during the trip. Such potpies as Italian Picnic Potpie (page 54), Joe's Special Potpie (page 77), and Quick Choucroute Potpie (page 93) are good examples. Plan to bake them at home and reheat them, if necessary, when you arrive. Fit the baking container into a basket or container that will hold the potpie safely in place during transport.

Freezing Many potpies that have a cooked filling and a crust topping can be assembled, frozen, and baked later. Those that work well for making ahead and freezing are noted in the recipes. To freeze an unbaked potpie, use a baking container that can go safely from refrigerator to oven. Chill the unbaked potpie in the refrigerator, wrap it tightly in plastic wrap and heavy aluminum foil, and freeze it for up to 1 month. Defrost the covered potpie in the refrigerator, preferably overnight. Uncover the dish and bake the potpie, but allow at least 5 additional minutes of baking time.

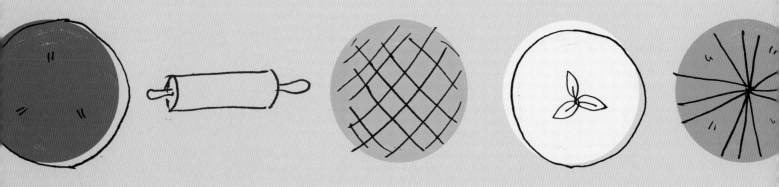

Three crusts are used repeatedly for these potpie recipes: a basic flaky pie crust, a tender cream cheese crust, and a sour cream crust that mimics the buttery layers characteristic of puff pastry.

All three crusts can be mixed in several minutes with an electric mixer. The doughs for the flaky crust and sour cream crust use cold butter and have a mixing method that allows bits of butter to remain in the dough. These butter pieces help form the flaky layers of the baked crusts. Soft butter is mixed into the cream cheese dough, and the result is an extremely tender cookie-type crust.

Some crusts go well with a particular kind of potpie. The flaky crust works with down-to-earth Grandma Tillie's Swiss Steak Potpie (page 74), Mediterranean Fish Stew Potpie (page 78), and Basque Chicken Pipérade Potpie (page 98). Rich and sophisticated Italian Easter Potpie (page 53), Lobster Potpie (page 61), and Salmon Coulibiac Potpie (page 65) pair well with the sour cream pastry crust. Lighter vegetable potpies are a natural companion for the tender cream cheese crust. Still, these crusts are interchangeable. If you have a favorite, don't hesitate to use it instead of the suggested one.

Crusts should be pressed firmly onto the edge of baking dishes. They can be fluted like a regular pie crust or simply pressed onto the rim of the baking dish with the tines of a fork. Dough scraps can be rolled into a rope and pressed decoratively around the sealed edge, or rolled out and cut with a cookie cutter to decorate the top of the pie. Autumn-vegetable potpies can have a leaf decoration, mushroom potpies a mushroom, or lobster potpies a lobster.

An egg wash will give a shiny golden finish to a crust. A basic egg wash formula is 1 egg beaten with 2 tablespoons heavy whipping cream. Brush the crust, not the fluted edge, with egg wash before putting it into the oven. You will not use all of the egg wash on one crust, but it is best to discard any that is left over.

YOU-CAN-DO-IT FLAKY CRUST

Makes enough dough to top a 9- or 10-inch round or square baking container or 4 individual containers

1 cup unbleached all-purpose flour

1/3 cup cake flour

2 teaspoons sugar

1/4 teaspoon salt

5 tablespoons cold unsalted butter, cut into 1/2-inch pieces

3 tablespoons cold vegetable shortening, cut into 3/4-inch pieces

31/2 to 4 tablespoons ice water

Each of the ingredients in this recipe helps to make a consistently successful crust. The butter adds flavor and the vegetable shortening adds flakiness. The lower gluten content of the cake flour, added to the all-purpose flour, helps make the crust tender. A bit of sugar and salt enhance the flavor. Cold water keeps the butter and shortening from softening so the fat can form the little pockets in the crust that make it flaky. You can make this crust in an electric mixer, a food processor, or by hand. On a warm humid day, this crust will probably need less water. The rolling and baking directions are given in each specific potpie recipe.

~~~~~~~~~~~~~~~

1. **To make the pastry in an electric mixer:** In the large bowl of an electric mixer on low speed, mix the flours, sugar, and salt for a few seconds to blend them. Stop the mixer, add the butter and shortening, then continue mixing just until the largest pieces are the size of small lima beans, about 20 seconds. They will not all be the same size, and you will still see loose flour. Slowly add the water, 1 tablespoon at a time. Stop mixing as soon as the mixture begins to hold together, about 20 seconds. The dough will form large clumps and pull away from the sides of the bowl, but will not form a ball. It is fine to stop the mixer at any time and squeeze a small piece of dough to check to see if it holds together.

To make the pastry in a food processor: Put the flours, sugar, and salt in a food processor and pulse several times to blend them. Add the butter pieces and shortening, pulsing just until the largest pieces are about 1/2 inch in size. Gradually add 3 tablespoons of the water and pulse, adding additional water just until the dough begins to come together in a mass but does not form a ball.

MIXING TIME: ABOUT 3 MINUTES

Continued

To make the pastry by hand: In a large bowl, stir the flours, sugar, and salt together to blend them. Add the butter pieces and shortening and, using your fingertips, a pastry blender, or 2 dinner knives, cut them into the flour mixture until the largest pieces are about the size of small lima beans. Gradually sprinkle 3 1/2 tablespoons of water over the mixture, stirring with a fork until it is evenly moistened and begins to come together in a mass. Add more water by teaspoons, if necessary. Gather the dough into a ball.

2. Turn the dough mixture out onto a lightly floured surface. With the heel of your hand, push the dough down and forward against the surface. Fold the dough in half and repeat 6 times. The dough will look smooth. Form the dough into a disk about 6 inches in diameter. It will be easier to roll neatly if the edges are smooth, but don't handle it a lot. Wrap the dough in plastic wrap and chill it in the refrigerator for at least 20 minutes or as long as overnight. The dough is now ready to roll.

SUREFIRE CREAM CHEESE CRUST

Makes enough dough for a 9- or 10-inch round or square baking container or 4 individual dishes

1 cup unbleached all-purpose flour

¼ teaspoon salt

½ cup (1 stick) unsalted butter, at room temperature

3 ounces cold cream cheese, cut into 3 pieces

Ease of mixing and tenderness are the main characteristics of this crust. It's as simple to prepare as the most basic cookie dough, and the result truly earns the right to be called foolproof. Using cold cream cheese produces a soft but not sticky dough. Cutting up the cream cheese makes it easier to blend.

MIXING TIME: ABOUT 2 MINUTES

———~~~~~~~———

1. Sift the flour and salt together into a small bowl and set aside. In a large bowl and using an electric mixer on low speed, beat the butter and cream cheese until smoothly blended, about 45 seconds. Mix in the flour mixture until the dough holds together and forms large clumps that come away from the sides of the bowl, about 30 seconds.

Or, use a large spoon to stir the butter and cream cheese together until smoothly blended, then add the flour and salt and continue stirring until clumps of smooth dough form.

2. Form the dough into a smooth ball, flatten it into a 6-inch disk, wrap it in plastic wrap, and refrigerate for 30 minutes or as long as overnight. The dough is now ready to roll and use in the recipes.

Steps Ahead: The dough can be refrigerated overnight, but it will have to sit at room temperature until it is soft enough to roll easily. This can take as long as 1 hour in a cool kitchen. The dough can be wrapped tightly in plastic wrap and aluminum foil and frozen for up to 1 month. Defrost the wrapped dough in the refrigerator overnight and let it sit at room temperature until it is soft enough to roll easily.

Variation: To make 2 crusts, double the ingredients.

EXTREMELY FLAKY SOUR CREAM CRUST

Makes enough dough for a 9- or 10-inch round or square baking container or 4 individual containers

MIXING TIME: ABOUT 3 MINUTES

1 cup unbleached all-purpose flour

1/2 teaspoon baking soda

1/4 teaspoon salt

1/2 cup (1 stick) cold unsalted butter, cut into 16 pieces

1/4 cup cold sour cream

This could also be called the "miracle crust." Flour, salt, butter, sour cream, and a little baking soda for extra lift are all it takes to make a dough that bakes into a crisp multilayered crust.

1. **To make the pastry in an electric mixer:** Sift the flour, baking soda, and salt into a large bowl. Add the butter pieces and mix them with an electric mixer on low speed until the largest of the butter pieces are the size of small lima beans, about 1 minute. The butter pieces will be different sizes and there will still be some loose flour. Add the sour cream and continue mixing until large clumps of smooth dough that pull away from the sides of the bowl form, about 30 seconds. Stop the mixer and scrape the beaters clean, if needed.

To make the pastry by hand: Sift the flour, baking soda, and salt into a large bowl. Use a pastry blender, your fingertips, or 2 dinner knives to combine the flour mixture and the butter until lima bean–size pieces form. Add the sour cream and stir with a large spoon for about 2 minutes until clumps of smooth dough form.

2. Form the dough into a smooth ball, flatten it into a 6-inch disk, wrap it in plastic wrap, and refrigerate for 30 to 60 minutes. You will see small pieces of butter in the dough. This is good and contributes to the flaky texture. The dough is now ready to roll and use in the recipes.

Steps Ahead: The dough can be refrigerated overnight, but it will have to sit at room temperature until it is soft enough to roll easily. This can take as long as 1 hour in a cool kitchen. The dough can be wrapped tightly in plastic wrap and aluminum foil and frozen for up to 1 month. Defrost the wrapped dough in the refrigerator overnight and let it sit at room temperature until soft enough to roll easily.

Variations: For decorating the top of a potpie with strips of pastry (see Salmon Coulibiac Potpie, page 65), make 1½ times the recipe, using 1½ cups unbleached all-purpose flour, ⅜ teaspoon salt, ¾ teaspoon baking soda, ¾ cup (1½ sticks) cold unsalted butter, and 6 tablespoons cold sour cream.

To make 2 crusts, double the ingredients.

Various flavorings can be stirred into the flour mixture before the butter is added. Try 1 teaspoon freshly ground black pepper, 2 teaspoons curry powder, or 2 teaspoons finely grated lemon zest.

TEN ESPECIALLY EASY POTPIES

These simple potpies are a good choice for a first foray into potpie making. They use easy-to-make crusts that do not need rolling, and fillings that require little or no precooking. On my busiest days, I look to these potpies for a good, fast dinner.

Phyllo pastry, tortillas, and rye bread crumbs are ready-made toppings. Dumplings, a cornmeal tamale, or a walnut crumble are toppings that can be stirred together quickly. Filling preparations consist of either just chopping a few ingredients or simply stirring them with seasonings and spreading them in a baking dish. The common denominator is potpies that are "as easy as pie."

CHILAQUILES POTPIE

One 14 1/2-ounce can whole tomatoes, drained

2 tablespoons corn or canola oil

2 cups coarsely chopped onions (2 medium)

3 cloves garlic, finely chopped

6 canned whole green chiles (two 3 1/2-ounce cans), drained, seeded, and coarsely chopped

2 fresh or canned jalapeño chiles, drained if canned, seeded, and finely chopped

10 corn tortillas, about 6 inches in diameter

Salt and freshly ground black pepper

1 cup (4 ounces) shredded sharp Cheddar cheese

1 cup (4 ounces) shredded Jack cheese

1/2 cup pitted black olives, halved

1 cup sour cream for serving (optional)

Chilaquiles is also known as "poor man's food," but this potpie based on that Mexican dish has nothing humble about it. Layers of green chiles, tomatoes, cheese, and seasonings are baked under a crisp circular-patterned layer of corn tortillas. I call it "every man's food."

Eggs, chorizo sausage, or cooked chicken can be added to this vegetarian version, and salsa can stand in for the tomatoes and chiles. Serve this potpie at the table, so everyone can see the attractive topping.

NOTE: When working with jalapeños or other hot chiles, be sure to wear clean rubber gloves and wash your hands afterward. This prevents any skin or eye irritation.

~~~~~~~~~~~~

1. Position a rack in the middle of the oven. Preheat the oven to 375°F. Have ready a baking dish with at least a 6-cup capacity. A rustic-looking ceramic baking dish makes a good choice.

2. Put the tomatoes on a plate, chop them coarsely, and set aside. In a large skillet, heat 1 tablespoon of the oil over medium heat for 1 minute. Add the onions and cook until they soften, about 5 minutes, stirring often. Stir in the garlic and continue cooking for another minute. Return the heat to medium-low and add the green and jalapeño chiles. Add the tomatoes and any of the juices that have accumulated on the plate, using a fork to break the tomatoes up into pieces. Continue cooking for 5 minutes, stirring constantly. Tear 7 of the tortillas into about 8 pieces each and add them to the pan. Cook for another minute, stirring to coat the tortilla pieces with the sauce. Remove the pan from the heat. Add salt and pepper to taste.

Continued

3. Spoon about $1/3$ of the tortilla mixture into the baking dish, spreading it evenly. Sprinkle about $1/3$ of the Cheddar and $1/3$ of the Jack cheese over it. Spoon all the olives evenly over the cheese. Repeat the tortilla and cheese layering twice, ending with the cheese layer. Brush the 3 remaining tortillas with the remaining 1 tablespoon oil. Use scissors to cut each tortilla into 8 wedges. Arrange the tortilla wedges in 2 overlapping circular rows to cover the cheese completely. Sprinkle the top generously with black pepper.

4. Bake until the filling is bubbling gently and the tortilla topping is lightly browned, especially on the edges, about 25 minutes. Serve immediately, with sour cream if desired.

BROCCOLI, BLUE CHEESE & WALNUT POTPIE

Filling

4 cups (about 1 pound) broccoli florets, cut into bite-size pieces

1 cup (4 ounces) walnuts

8 ounces blue cheese

2/3 cup whole milk

2 tablespoons fresh lemon juice

1/4 teaspoon freshly ground black pepper

Topping

1 cup unbleached all-purpose flour

1 tablespoon sugar

1/2 teaspoon salt

1/4 teaspoon freshly ground black pepper

4 tablespoons unsalted butter, melted

1 cup (4 ounces) finely chopped walnuts

It takes about 15 seconds for a food processor to whirl the walnuts and blue cheese filling to a thick sauce and not much longer to stir the crunchy walnut topping together. During baking, the sauce takes on a pâté consistency. This makes a good vegetarian choice for a light dinner or substantial side dish. Danish, Maytag, or Great Hill are all good blue cheese choices.

————~~~~~~~~~————

1. Position a rack in the middle of the oven. Preheat the oven to 375°F. Have ready a baking dish with a 6-cup capacity.

2. Make the filling: In a large saucepan, bring about 6 cups lightly salted water to a boil. Add the broccoli and cook, uncovered, for about 5 minutes until the broccoli tests tender with a fork. Drain in a colander and run cold water over the broccoli. This will help it keep a bright green color. Transfer the broccoli to a large bowl and set aside.

3. In a food processor, process the walnuts until finely ground. Some walnuts will be finely chopped. Add the blue cheese, milk, lemon juice, and pepper, processing on and off until smooth. You will see flecks of walnuts. Stir the blue cheese mixture into the broccoli to coat it evenly with sauce. Transfer all of the broccoli and sauce into the baking dish.

4. Prepare the topping: In a medium bowl, stir the flour, sugar, salt, and pepper together. Add the melted butter, stirring until the mixture is evenly moistened and forms crumbs. Stir in the walnuts. Spoon the topping evenly over the filling, pressing it gently to make an even layer.

5. Bake until the topping is lightly browned and the filling makes a sizzling sound, about 25 minutes. Use a large spoon to scoop out servings of crust and filling.

CHICKEN & PARSLEY DUMPLING POTPIE

Filling

4 tablespoons unsalted butter

1/4 cup unbleached all-purpose flour

4 cups chicken broth (low sodium if canned)

1 teaspoon fresh thyme leaves, or 1/2 teaspoon dried

3 cups cooked chicken, cut into 1-inch pieces (see page 14)

3 tablespoons finely chopped fresh chives

Salt and freshly ground pepper

Topping

6 tablespoons cornmeal

6 tablespoons unbleached all-purpose flour

1/2 teaspoon baking powder

1/4 teaspoon salt

2 tablespoons cold unsalted butter, cut into pieces

1/4 cup milk (any fat content)

1 large egg

2 tablespoons finely chopped fresh parsley

This is a true potpie. Both the chicken filling and the dumpling topping are cooked and served in the cooking pot. With chunks of cooked chicken bubbling in a broth-based sauce and quick-to-mix cornmeal dumplings steaming on top, this potpie defines comfort food. The fairly thin sauce thickens quite a bit when the dumpling topping cooks with it.

NOTE: Strain and save the broth from cooking the chicken (see page 14) to use for the sauce.

1. **Make the filling:** In a medium saucepan, melt the butter over low heat. As soon as the butter melts, add the flour and increase the heat to medium. Using a wooden spoon and stirring constantly, cook the butter and flour until it is bubbling and just beginning to become slightly golden, about 2 minutes. Using a whisk and whisking constantly, slowly pour in the chicken broth. Keep whisking until the sauce is smooth. Bring to a gentle boil, adjusting the heat as necessary, and cook for 5 minutes. The sauce will thicken slightly to the consistency of a thick syrup. Add the thyme and chicken pieces. Continue cooking, uncovered, to blend the flavors for 15 minutes, then add the chives, salt and pepper to taste. Make the dumpling batter while the chicken cooks in the sauce.

2. **Prepare the topping:** In a medium bowl, stir the cornmeal, flour, baking powder, and salt together. Using your fingertips, a fork, or a pastry blender, cut the butter pieces until they are the size of peas. You will still see loose flour. In a small bowl and using a fork, stir the milk and egg together. Use a spoon to stir the milk mixture and parsley into the cornmeal mixture, stirring just to evenly moisten the dry ingredients.

Continued

3. Drop rounded tablespoons of batter onto the gently bubbling filling. You will have 8 or 9 dumplings. Cover the saucepan and adjust the heat to keep the potpie at a gentle boil, and continue cooking until the dumplings are done, about 10 minutes. Use a knife to cut into one of the dumplings to make sure that they are firm throughout. The sauce will thicken considerably while the dumplings cook.

4. Remove the saucepan from the heat and spoon servings of dumpling and filling onto serving plates.

HOT CHICKEN SALAD POTPIE

Makes **6** servings

POTPIE BAKING: 375°F FOR ABOUT 15 MINUTES

Filling

2 boneless, skinless chicken breasts, cooked and cut into 3/4-inch pieces (see page 14)

2 cups finely chopped celery (about 5 stalks)

1/2 cup (2 ounces) slivered almonds, toasted (see page 13)

1 tablespoon grated onion

1 teaspoon grated lemon zest

2 tablespoons fresh lemon juice

1 cup mayonnaise

Topping

6 phyllo pastry sheets (about 13 by 17 inches), thawed if frozen

3 tablespoons unsalted butter, melted

1/2 teaspoon salt

Here is a recipe that has stood the test of time. Over thirty years ago, I had a hot turkey salad for lunch at the Allied Arts Guild restaurant in Menlo Park, California. It was staffed then, as now, by volunteers, with the proceeds going to help critically ill children at the Lucile Packard Children's Hospital. The restaurant sold copies of their recipes for twenty-five cents each (probably a little costlier now). That salad evolved into this chicken potpie with a crisp salted phyllo topping. The phyllo pastry is crumpled into loose balls for an especially crisp result.

————～～～～～～～————

1. Position a rack in the middle of the oven. Preheat the oven to 375°F. Have ready a 9-by-2-inch round baking dish or glass pie dish.

2. Make the filling: In a large bowl and using a large spoon, mix the filling ingredients together just to distribute them evenly and coat the chicken pieces with mayonnaise. Spoon the filling into the baking dish, spreading it evenly.

3. Prepare the topping: Lay out the phyllo pastry sheets in a stack. Immediately cover them completely with a damp dish towel. Use plastic wrap to roll up and tightly rewrap any leftover phyllo and refrigerate it for up to 1 week. Spread 1 sheet of phyllo on the counter and use a pastry brush to brush it lightly with butter, then sprinkle it lightly with salt. Crumple it up lightly into a loose ball (like a piece of newspaper) and place it on the filling. If any phyllo breaks off, just put it back on the ball of pastry. Repeat with the remaining 5 sheets of phyllo, arranging it to cover the filling. You will have 6 bundles of phyllo covering the filling.

4. Bake just until the phyllo topping is golden and the filling hot, about 15 minutes. This filling bakes for a short time, so that the celery in the filling remains crisp. Use a spoon to serve the filling and 1 phyllo bundle for each serving.

GREEK THREE-CHEESE, SPINACH & ONION POTPIE

Makes **12** servings

COOKING THE FILLING:
5 MINUTES

POTPIE BAKING:
350°F FOR ABOUT
45 MINUTES

6 phyllo pastry sheets (about 13 by 17 inches), thawed if previously frozen

Filling

1 tablespoon olive oil

2 cups finely chopped onions (2 medium)

Two 10-ounce packages thawed frozen chopped spinach

One 15- or 16-ounce container ricotta cheese (2 cups); part skim is fine

8 ounces feta cheese, crumbled (1½ cups)

2 cups (8 ounces) shredded Jack cheese

2 large eggs

3 tablespoons finely chopped fresh dill

3 tablespoons finely chopped fresh parsley

¼ teaspoon salt

¼ teaspoon freshly ground black pepper

3 tablespoons unsalted butter, melted

My potpie version of the Greek cheese and spinach turnover called spanakopita loads the traditional filling with ricotta, feta, and Jack cheese, fresh dill and parsley, and uses store-bought phyllo pastry for the crisp topping. Its generous size and do-ahead preparation make it an ideal party dish. To serve a really big crowd, double the ingredients and bake it in two baking dishes. It is easy to keep phyllo pastry soft and pliable as long as it is carefully covered with a damp dish towel while you are working with it.

———~~~~~~~~~~———

1. Position a rack in the middle of the oven. Preheat the oven to 350°F. Butter a 9-by-13-by-2-inch baking dish.

2. Lay out the phyllo pastry sheets and stack them. Use plastic wrap to roll up and tightly rewrap any leftover phyllo and refrigerate it for up to 1 week. Using the bottom of the baking dish as a guide, use kitchen scissors to cut 6 pieces of phyllo that are 1 inch larger all around than the baking dish. Immediately cover the cut sheets of phyllo completely with a damp dish towel. Set aside while you make the filling.

3. **Make the filling:** In a medium skillet, heat the olive oil over medium heat for about 1 minute. Add the onions and cook until they soften, about 5 minutes, stirring often. Set aside.

4. Rest a strainer over a medium bowl, put the spinach in the strainer, and use a large spoon to press firmly on the spinach to press out the liquid. Discard the liquid.

Continued

5. In a large bowl and using a large spoon, stir the onions, drained spinach, ricotta, feta, Jack cheese, eggs, dill, parsley, salt, and pepper together to combine them. Spread half of the filling in the baking dish. Place 2 pieces of the phyllo pastry on top of the filling in the dish. Brush the pastry lightly with melted butter. Top with one more piece of phyllo. Tuck any overhanging edges under to form a smooth edge that neatly covers the filling. Spread the remaining filling over the phyllo. Top with 2 more pieces of phyllo and brush them lightly with butter. Top with the remaining phyllo sheet and brush it with butter. Use a sharp knife to mark 12 squares by cutting through the top layers of pastry.

6. Bake until the topping is golden and the filling is bubbling gently, about 45 minutes. Use a sharp knife to cut through the marked squares and a spatula with a wide blade to remove and serve the squares.

TAMALE POTPIE

Makes **8** servings

COOKING THE FILLING:
16 MINUTES

POTPIE BAKING:
375°F FOR ABOUT
35 MINUTES

Filling

1 tablespoon corn or canola oil

1 cup coarsely chopped onion
(1 medium)

1 cup coarsely chopped green
bell pepper (1 medium)

2 cloves garlic, finely chopped

1 pound lean ground pork

1/2 teaspoon ground cumin

3 tablespoons chili powder

1/4 teaspoon salt or to taste

One 14 1/2-ounce can tomatoes
in their own juice

Topping

1 cup cornmeal

1/4 teaspoon salt

3/4 cup chicken broth
(low sodium if canned)

1 large egg

1 tablespoon corn or canola oil

1 cup sour cream for serving (optional)

1/4 cup chopped fresh cilantro
for serving (optional)

Mixing chicken broth and cornmeal together creates a tamale-like topping that is one of the easiest "crusts" you will ever stir together. It has a mild flavor and dense texture that makes a good foil to the spicy, moist ground pork filling.

NOTE: Chili powder loses its flavor quickly, so it is always a good idea to taste it to make sure that it is fresh and pungent.

1. Position a rack in the middle of the oven. Preheat the oven to 375°F. Have ready a 9-by-2-inch round baking dish or glass pie dish.

2. Make the filling: In a large skillet, heat the oil over medium heat for 1 minute. Add the onion, bell pepper, and garlic and cook until the vegetables soften, about 10 minutes, stirring often. Add the ground pork and cook, stirring with a fork to break up any clumps, until it is no longer pink. If necessary, carefully pour off any excess fat and discard it. Stir in the cumin, chili powder, and salt. Add the tomatoes with their juice, stirring them with a fork to break them up into pieces about 3/4 inch in size. Cook, uncovered, on low heat for 5 minutes, stirring often. Spoon the filling into the baking dish and let it cool for about 15 minutes.

3. Prepare the topping: In a medium bowl, use a large spoon to stir the cornmeal and salt together. In a small bowl, stir the chicken broth, egg, and oil together. Pour the liquid over the cornmeal and stir just until it is evenly moistened and forms a thin, pourable batter. Pour the topping over the filling in the baking dish, spreading it evenly.

4. Bake until the topping is lightly browned and feels firm, and the filling is gently bubbling, about 35 minutes. Use a sharp knife to cut the topping into wedges and serve, with sour cream and cilantro, if desired.

INDIVIDUAL SHRIMP SCAMPI POTPIES

Filling

1 pound medium-size raw shrimp, peeled and deveined

1/4 cup fresh lemon juice

2 tablespoons chopped fresh basil

1 tablespoon finely chopped fresh parsley

3 cloves garlic, finely chopped

2 tablespoons olive oil

1/8 teaspoon salt

1/8 teaspoon freshly ground black pepper

Topping

2 cups panko (Japanese bread crumbs)

6 tablespoons unsalted butter, melted

Lemon, basil, and garlic are a made-for-each other seasoning combination that goes perfectly with shrimp scampi. Japanese-style panko are large crumbs that produce a crisp, crustlike topping.

1. Position a rack in the middle of the oven. Preheat the oven to 400°F. Put 4 ovenproof baking dishes or ovenproof bowls with a 2-cup capacity on a baking sheet. The sheet makes it easier to move the baking dishes in and out of the oven.

2. **Make the filling:** Rinse the shrimp with cold water and pat dry with paper towels. In a medium bowl, stir the shrimp, lemon juice, basil, parsley, garlic, olive oil, salt, and pepper together to coat the shrimp evenly. Divide the mixture evenly among the 4 baking dishes.

3. **Prepare the topping:** In a medium bowl, stir the panko and butter together to evenly moisten the crumbs. Dividing the mixture evenly, spoon about 1/2 cup of it evenly over the shrimp in each baking dish. Pat the crumbs gently to form a firm, even coating.

4. Bake until the topping is lightly browned and the juices are bubbling, about 15 minutes. The shrimp will be pink. Protecting your hands with pot holders, put the hot baking dishes on individual plates and serve.

REUBEN POTPIE

Topping

6 slices seeded rye bread
(day old is fine)

1/4 cup shredded Swiss cheese

6 tablespoons unsalted butter, melted

Filling

6 ounces corned beef or pastrami,
trimmed of all fat

1 cup (4 ounces) shredded Swiss cheese

1 cup (4 ounces) shredded sharp
Cheddar cheese

1 pound (about 4 cups) fresh
sauerkraut, drained

1/2 cup mayonnaise (light is fine)

2 tablespoons caraway seed

A Step Ahead: The potpie can be
assembled early in the day and baked
later. Cover and refrigerate it until baking
time and plan on an additional 5 minutes
of time to bake it.

This Reuben in a potpie goes together as fast as a sandwich. Corned beef is the traditional meat, but pastrami works as well and adds a bit more spice. It is best to buy the sauerkraut that comes in jars in the refrigerated section of supermarkets or fresh sauerkraut from a local deli. A great source for fresh barrel-cured sauerkraut that is reasonably priced is Morse's Sauerkraut in Waldoboro, Maine (see Sources, page 130). Canned sauerkraut is softer and does not work as well.

1. Position a rack in the middle of the oven. Preheat the oven to 375°F. Have ready a baking dish with an 8-cup capacity.

2. Prepare the topping: Tear the rye bread slices into approximately 2-inch pieces and process them in a food processor to form coarse crumbs, about 15 seconds. Measure 4 cups crumbs and put them in a medium bowl. Save any remaining crumbs for another use. Stir in the Swiss cheese, then the melted butter to evenly moisten the crumbs. Set aside. The next step will be to shred the corned beef in the food processor, but it is not necessary to clean the work bowl after processing the bread crumbs.

3. Make the filling: Cut the corned beef into approximately 1-inch pieces. Pulse to process the corned beef in the food processor until coarsely shredded. In a large bowl, use a large fork to stir the corned beef, Swiss cheese, Cheddar cheese, sauerkraut, mayonnaise, and caraway seed together. Spoon the filling into the baking dish. Spoon the crumb topping over the filling and pat the crumbs gently to form an even coating.

4. Bake until the topping is lightly browned and the filling makes a sizzling sound, about 35 minutes. Use a large spoon to scoop out servings of crust and filling.

DILLED CRABMEAT POTPIE WITH PHYLLO CRUST

Filling

1 pound fresh lump crabmeat, picked over for shell

1/2 cup mayonnaise (light is fine)

1 teaspoon finely grated lemon zest

2 tablespoons fresh lemon juice

1/4 cup lightly packed chopped fresh dill leaves

Topping

6 phyllo pastry sheets (about 13 by 17 inches), thawed if frozen

2 tablespoons unsalted butter, melted

Salt and freshly ground black pepper

A Step Ahead: The potpie can be assembled up to 6 hours ahead, covered with plastic wrap, and refrigerated. Remove the covered container from the refrigerator 15 minutes before baking. Remove the plastic wrap just before the potpie goes into the oven. Bake for about 5 additional minutes.

Crisp phyllo pastry sprinkled with salt and pepper makes a quick potpie topping. When working with sheets of phyllo pastry, be sure to keep them covered with a damp dish towel, to keep them soft and pliable.

————〰〰〰〰〰————

1. Position a rack in the middle of the oven. Preheat the oven to 375°F. Have ready a 9-by-2-inch round ovenproof ceramic baking dish or glass pie dish.

2. Make the filling: In a large bowl, gently stir the crabmeat, mayonnaise, lemon zest, lemon juice, and dill together just until they are evenly mixed. Spread the crab mixture in the baking container.

3. Prepare the topping: Spread out the phyllo sheets in a stack. Rewrap leftover phyllo and refrigerate. Using the top of the baking dish as a guide and kitchen scissors, cut 6 circles that are 1 inch larger in diameter than the top of the container. Immediately cover the phyllo completely with a damp dish towel.

4. Place 2 of the phyllo circles on top of the filling in the dish. Brush the pastry lightly with melted butter then sprinkle it lightly with salt and pepper. The edges of the pastry will hang slightly over the edge of the container. Add another 2 phyllo circles and brush them lightly with melted butter. Top with the remaining 2 phyllo circles, brush the pastry with butter, and sprinkle it lightly with salt and pepper. Fold the overhanging edges of pastry under to form a smooth edge that neatly covers the filling. Use a sharp knife to mark 8 wedges by cutting through the top layers of pastry. Bake until the pastry is golden, about 20 minutes.

5. Use a sharp knife to cut through the previously marked pieces of phyllo pastry. Use a large spoon or spatula to lift the wedges onto serving plates. Replace any crust that slides off the filling.

DEVILED CRAB POTPIE

Makes **8** appetizer or **4** entrée servings

COOKING THE FILLING:
6 MINUTES

POTPIE BAKING:
375°F FOR ABOUT
15 MINUTES

Filling

1 pound fresh lump crabmeat,
picked over for shell

1/4 cup mayonnaise

1 tablespoon unsalted butter

1/2 cup finely chopped onion
(1/2 medium)

1/2 cup finely chopped celery

1/4 cup finely chopped red bell pepper

1 tablespoon finely chopped
fresh parsley

1 teaspoon finely grated lemon zest

2 tablespoons fresh lemon juice

1 teaspoon paprika
(sweet Hungarian preferred)

2 teaspoons Worcestershire sauce

Salt and freshly ground black pepper

Topping

1 1/2 cups panko
(Japanese bread crumbs)

1 teaspoon paprika
(sweet Hungarian preferred)

4 tablespoons unsalted butter, melted

A fancy lunch, sophisticated first course, or main dish, this potpie fits in anywhere and into any busy schedule. Preparation consists of a quick cooking to soften the vegetables and then simply stirring the ingredients together. Baking time is a mere 15 minutes, and it is ready to serve.

1. Position a rack in the middle of the oven. Preheat the oven to 375°F. Put 4 ovenproof baking dishes or ovenproof bowls with a 2-cup capacity (for entrées) or 8 ramekins with a 1-cup capacity (for appetizers) on a baking sheet. The baking sheet makes it easier to move the baking dishes in and out of the oven.

2. Make the filling: In a medium bowl, stir the crabmeat and mayonnaise together. Set aside.

3. In a medium skillet, melt the butter over medium heat for 1 minute. Add the onion, celery, and bell pepper and cook until they soften, about 5 minutes, stirring often. Remove the pan from the heat and set aside. Stir the parsley, lemon zest, lemon juice, paprika, and Worcestershire into the crabmeat. Stir in the onion mixture. Season with salt and pepper. Divide the filling evenly among the baking dishes.

4. Prepare the topping: In a medium bowl, stir the panko, paprika, and melted butter together to evenly moisten the panko. Divide the mixture evenly among the filled baking containers. Pat gently to form a firm, even coating over the crabmeat.

5. Bake until the topping is lightly browned and the juices are bubbling gently, about 15 minutes. Protecting your hands with pot holders, put the hot baking dishes on individual plates and serve.

A WORLD of POTPIE CLASSICS

I do not think that I have seen the term *potpie* used in other countries, but the potpie as we know it exists all over the world. There is the cheese, prosciutto, and spinach pie served for Easter in Italy; that British favorite, cottage pie; and Russian coulibiac of salmon. All of them are popular potpie favorites. They have the required topping, sometimes crusty and sometimes as soft as mashed potatoes, plus a moist filling.

Chicken potpie could be considered the American classic potpie. But substituting a curry sauce transports the idea to an international level. In South America (especially Argentina), there are many empanada stands selling hand-held meat-filled pies, so this potpie becomes an individual meal. The French spiced beef pie topped with mashed potatoes, known as *hachis Parmentier,* needs no alterations to be considered potpie fare. All of these potpies represent home cooking the world over.

FARMERS' MARKET CHICKEN POTPIE

Crust

1 1/2 cups unbleached all-purpose flour

1/2 teaspoon salt

1/2 cup cold vegetable shortening, cut into 8 pieces

4 to 5 tablespoons ice water

Filling

5 tablespoons unbleached all-purpose flour

1/2 cup water

3 cups chicken broth (low sodium if canned)

1 tablespoon chicken soup base (low sodium preferred)

4 cups cooked chicken, cut into 1-inch pieces (see page 14)

1 cup thawed frozen peas

Salt and freshly ground black pepper

When most people think of potpie, it is chicken potpie that comes to mind. So the one that I chose to include had to be a "best in its class" example. There was no question that my favorite pie was John Barstein's chicken potpie that I had been buying for years at our local farmers' market. John owns Maine-ly Poultry in Warren, Maine, and raises his own chickens. His potpie has large, moist chunks of chicken (white or mixed, as you prefer), peas if you want, a chicken broth gravy (John correctly calls it gravy, not sauce), and an old-fashioned flaky crust. One morning at the market, John generously shared the recipe with me, so I could have this treasure to pass along.

⸻〰〰〰〰〰⸻

1. **Make the crust:** In a large bowl, using a large spoon, stir the flour and salt together. Stir in the shortening pieces just to coat them with flour. Use a pastry blender or 2 dinner knives to cut in the shortening until fine crumbs form, with the largest only 1/4 inch in size. Sprinkle 4 tablespoons of the water over the mixture, stirring with a fork until it is evenly moistened and begins to come together in a mass. Add the 1 tablespoon additional water by teaspoons, if necessary. The more humid the day, the less water will be needed.

2. Turn the dough mixture out onto a lightly floured rolling surface. With the heel of your hand, push the dough down and forward against the surface several times until it looks smooth. Form the dough into a disk about 6 inches in diameter. It will be easier to roll into a circle if the edges are smooth, but don't handle it a lot. Wrap the dough in plastic wrap and refrigerate for at least 30 minutes or as long as overnight. If chilled overnight, the dough will have to sit at room temperature for 15 to 30 minutes (depending on the kitchen temperature) until it is soft enough to roll.

Steps Ahead: The potpie can be assembled and frozen before it is baked. Use a baking dish that can safely go from the refrigerator into a hot oven. To freeze it, wrap the potpie tightly in plastic wrap and heavy aluminum foil and refrigerate it for at least 1 hour, so that it is cold when it goes into the freezer. Freeze for up to 1 month. Defrost the wrapped potpie in the refrigerator; overnight is fine. Bake at 400°F for about 35 minutes, or until the crust is lightly browned and the hot filling is just beginning to bubble gently.

Crust Options: You-Can-Do-It Flaky Crust (page 19) can be used for this potpie. Or, use a store-bought refrigerated pie crust.

3. Position an oven rack in the middle of the oven. Preheat the oven to 400°F. Have ready a baking dish with a 6-cup capacity.

4. Make the filling: In a small bowl, stir the flour and water together until smooth. (John says that it should have the consistency of maple syrup.) Set aside. In a large saucepan over medium heat, heat the broth and soup base until it is hot and steam begins to rise from it, about 5 minutes. Whisk in the flour mixture, whisking constantly until it is smoothly incorporated. Bring to a gentle boil, adjusting the heat as necessary, and boil for 1 minute. The sauce will begin to thicken slightly to the consistency of a thick syrup. Add the chicken pieces. Continue cooking, uncovered, for about 5 minutes to blend the flavors and slightly thicken the gravy further. Stir in the peas and season with salt and pepper. Add salt sparingly since the soup base will probably have some salt. Transfer the filling to the baking dish. Set aside to cool for about 15 minutes while you roll the crust.

5. Lightly flour the rolling surface and rolling pin. Roll the dough to a shape that is 1 inch larger than the top of the baking dish. Roll the crust around the rolling pin and unroll it over the top of the baking dish. Fold ½ inch of the edge of the crust under to form a smooth edge. Use your thumb and forefinger to pinch the edge into a fluted or scalloped pattern around the inside edge of the dish while pressing it firmly onto the rim. Cut four 2-inch-long slits in the top of the crust to release steam while the pie bakes.

6. Bake for about 30 minutes, or until the crust is lightly browned and the filling is just beginning to bubble gently. Let rest for 5 minutes, then use a large spoon to cut down through the crust and scoop out servings of crust, gravy, and chicken.

CHICKEN CURRY POTPIE

Makes **6** servings

COOKING THE FILLING:
35 MINUTES

POTPIE BAKING:
375°F FOR ABOUT
30 MINUTES

1 pound boneless, skinless chicken breasts, cut into 1-inch pieces

Salt and freshly ground black pepper

2 tablespoons ghee or corn or canola oil

2 cups finely chopped onions (2 medium)

2 cloves garlic, finely chopped

6 slices peeled fresh ginger root, about 1/4 inch thick

1 teaspoon ground cumin

1 teaspoon ground coriander

1 teaspoon curry powder or more to taste

1/4 teaspoon cayenne pepper or hot paprika

One 14 1/2-ounce can whole tomatoes, drained

3/4 cup water

1/2 cup plain whole-milk yogurt

2 tablespoons heavy whipping cream

Surefire Cream Cheese Crust (page 21)

2 tablespoons chopped fresh cilantro leaves

Chicken curry may sound exotic for a potpie filling, but this curry simply seasons pieces of boneless chicken breast with Indian spices and cooks them quickly with some liquid and tomatoes. The exquisite result is a gorgeous golden filling that makes a colorful "dinner party" potpie.

I prefer to sauté the chicken in ghee, but corn or canola oil can be substituted. Ghee, which is actually clarified butter, does not burn easily, and adds a nutty browned-butter flavor. King Arthur Flour Baker's Catalogue (see Sources, page 130) sells ghee. Be sure to use whole-milk yogurt for the sauce, which is more like a rich, thick Indian yogurt. Serve the potpie with a scattering of cilantro leaves for a fresh, colorful finish. For a larger crowd, prepare 2 crusts and double the filling ingredients to make 2 potpies in 2 baking dishes.

---

1. Have ready a baking dish with a 6-cup capacity. Pat the chicken pieces dry with a paper towel and sprinkle them lightly with salt and pepper. In a large skillet, heat the ghee or oil over medium-high heat for 1 minute. Add the chicken pieces and use tongs to turn the chicken once to lightly brown on both sides, about 5 minutes. The chicken is not fully cooked at this point. Remove the chicken to a clean plate and set aside.

2. Reduce the heat to medium and add the onions, garlic, and ginger to the skillet. Cook until the onions soften and the edges begin to brown, about 6 minutes, stirring often. Stir in the cumin, coriander, curry powder, and cayenne or paprika, stirring to blend the spices. Add the tomatoes and use a fork to break them up into pieces about 3/4 inch in size. Pour in the water and return the chicken and any accumulated juices to the pan. Cover and cook on low heat at a gentle simmer, stirring occasionally, until the chicken pieces are no longer pink in the center, about 20 minutes.

Continued

3. Remove the pan from the heat and remove the ginger slices and discard them. Put the yogurt and cream in a small bowl and whisk in about $1/2$ cup of the warm liquid from the pan. Stir the yogurt mixture into the chicken curry to blend it into the sauce. Taste the sauce and add additional curry powder, if desired. Transfer the filling to the baking dish and let it cool for about 15 minutes while you roll the crust. Or, cover the filling with plastic wrap and refrigerate it for up to 1 day.

4. Position a rack in the middle of the oven. Preheat the oven to 375°F.

5. Lightly flour the rolling surface and rolling pin. Roll the crust dough to a shape that is 1 inch larger than the top of the baking dish. Roll the crust around the rolling pin and unroll it over the cooled chicken filling. Fold $1/2$ inch of the edge of the crust under to form a smooth edge. Use fork tines to press the dough firmly onto the rim of the baking dish. Cut four 2-inch-long slits in the top of the crust to release steam while the pie bakes.

6. Bake for about 30 minutes, or until the crust is lightly browned. Let rest for 5 minutes, then use a large spoon to cut down through the crust and scoop out servings of crust and filling. Sprinkle with the cilantro and serve.

INDIVIDUAL EMPANADA POTPIES

Filling

1 tablespoon olive oil

1/2 cup beef or chicken broth (low sodium if canned)

2 cups finely chopped onions (2 medium)

1 pound lean ground beef

1 jalapeño chile, finely chopped, or 1 teaspoon red pepper flakes

1 tablespoon paprika (sweet Hungarian preferred)

1/2 teaspoon ground cumin

1/2 teaspoon salt

1/4 teaspoon freshly ground black pepper

1/4 cup pitted black olives, finely chopped

2 tablespoons chopped fresh cilantro leaves

Topping

Surefire Cream Cheese Crust (page 21)

1 teaspoon paprika (sweet Hungarian preferred)

1 tablespoon milk

An empanada is a South American or Spanish turnover with a spicy (more common) or sweet filling. These individual empanada potpies have a ground beef and onion filling. The unique method of cooking the onions in broth gives them a soft, rather creamy consistency that carries over to the appealing texture of the filling.

~~~~~~~~~~~~~~~~~

1. Position a rack in the middle of the oven. Preheat the oven to 400°F. Put 4 ovenproof baking dishes or ovenproof bowls with a 2-cup capacity on a baking sheet. The baking sheet makes it easier to move the baking dishes in and out of the oven.

2. **Make the filling:** In a medium skillet, heat the oil and broth over medium-high heat for 1 minute. Add the onions and cook, uncovered, until the onions soften, about 5 minutes. Adjust the heat to keep the liquid gently bubbling. Add the ground beef and cook, stirring with a fork to break up any clumps, until it is no longer pink and any meat juices evaporate, about 10 minutes. Stir in the jalapeño or red pepper flakes, paprika, cumin, salt, and black pepper and cook for about 3 more minutes to blend the flavors, stirring often. Divide evenly among the 4 baking dishes. Sprinkle the olives and cilantro over the top of each. Set aside to cool slightly while you roll the crust.

3. **Prepare the topping:** Cut the crust dough into 4 equal pieces, one for each potpie. Lightly flour the rolling surface and rolling pin. Roll one piece of dough to a shape that is 3/4 inch larger than the top of the baking dish. Roll the crust around the rolling pin and unroll it over the filling. Fold 1/2 inch of the edge of the crust under to form a smooth edge. Use the tines of a fork to press the dough firmly onto the edge of the dish. Hold the fork at an angle to the edge to

Continued

produce a nice pattern. Repeat with the remaining 3 baking dishes. Sprinkle the paprika lightly over the top of each, then use a pastry brush to brush the top of each crust lightly with milk. Cut two 2-inch-long slits in the top of the crust to release steam while the potpies bake.

4. Bake for about 30 minutes, or until the crust is lightly browned and the filling is beginning to bubble gently. Protecting your hands with pot holders, put the hot baking dishes on individual plates and serve.

ITALIAN EASTER POTPIE

Filling

One 10-ounce package thawed frozen chopped spinach

2 cups (16 ounces) whole-milk ricotta cheese

2 cups (8 ounces) shredded fresh mozzarella cheese

2 large eggs

1 cup (4 ounces) freshly grated Parmesan cheese (Parmigiano-Reggiano preferred)

2 ounces prosciutto, thinly sliced and coarsely chopped

1/4 teaspoon salt

1/4 teaspoon freshly ground black pepper

Topping

Extremely Flaky Sour Cream Crust (page 22)

1 large egg beaten with 2 tablespoons heavy whipping cream for egg wash

2 tablespoons freshly grated Parmesan cheese (Parmigiano-Reggiano preferred)

Variation: Two ounces thinly sliced salami, cut into 1/4-inch strips, can be substituted for the prosciutto or added with it to the filling.

Crust Options: You-Can-Do-It Flaky Crust (page 19) or Surefire Cream Cheese Crust (page 21) can be used for this potpie. Or, use thawed frozen puff pastry.

Our Italian group does study Italian, but more often than not we talk about food. Of course, that is very Italian. During one of our "lessons," our teacher, Anna Mauri, gave us the *ricetta* for her *torta Pasqualina*—Easter pie. The ingredients are basic Italian ones: ricotta, Parmesan, spinach, prosciutto, and eggs baked with a puff-pastry-type crust. It is as simple as that, and a lovely way to celebrate Easter or spring or nothing.

—————~~~~~~~~~~~—————

1. Position a rack in the middle of the oven. Preheat the oven to 375°F. Rub a 9-by-2-inch round baking dish or glass pie dish with olive oil.

2. Make the filling: Rest a strainer over a medium bowl, put the spinach in the strainer, and push firmly on the spinach with a large spoon to press out the liquid. Discard the liquid. Set aside.

3. In a large bowl, stir the ricotta, mozzarella, eggs, drained spinach, Parmesan, prosciutto, salt, and pepper together. Spread the filling in the baking dish.

4. Prepare the topping: Lightly flour the rolling surface and rolling pin. Roll the crust dough to a shape that is about 1 1/2 inches larger than the top of the baking dish. Roll the crust around the rolling pin and unroll it over the top of the baking dish. Fold 3/4 inch of the edge of the crust under to form a smooth edge. Use your thumb and forefinger to pinch the edge into a scalloped pattern or fluted edge around the edge of the dish, while pressing it firmly onto the rim. Use a pastry brush to brush the top of the dough lightly with the egg wash. Cut four 2-inch-long slits in the top of the crust to release steam while the potpie bakes.

5. Bake for 30 minutes, then sprinkle with the 2 tablespoons of Parmesan cheese. Continue baking for about 10 more minutes, or until the crust is lightly browned. Let rest for 5 minutes, then use a large knife to cut wedges of crust and filling.

ITALIAN PICNIC POTPIE

Filling

Two 10-ounce packages thawed frozen chopped spinach

3 tablespoons plus 1 teaspoon olive oil

3 cloves garlic, finely chopped

Salt and freshly ground black pepper

1/2 pound thinly sliced baked ham

3/4 pound thinly sliced provolone cheese

1/4 pound thinly sliced Genoa salami

4 large pieces roasted red bell peppers (about 5 ounces)

Topping

Extremely Flaky Sour Cream Crust (page 22)

2 tablespoons heavy whipping cream beaten with 1 large egg for egg wash

Think of this as a loaded-with-filling submarine sandwich, but one that is assembled and baked as a potpie. That will give you some idea of what happens when the layers of ham, cheese, salami, spinach, and sweet peppers melt together in this Italian-inspired dish. Although fine served hot, this potpie is even better when served at room temperature, making it a good picnic choice. Buy a jar of good-quality roasted red peppers at the supermarket, or look for them at the deli counter.

———〰〰〰〰〰〰———

1. Preheat the oven to 375°F. Rub 1 teaspoon olive oil in the bottom of a 9-inch square baking dish that is 2 inches deep.

2. Make the filling: Rest a strainer over a medium bowl, put the spinach in the strainer, and push firmly on the spinach with a large spoon to press out the liquid. Discard the liquid. In a medium skillet, heat the 3 tablespoons olive oil over medium heat for about 1 minute. Add the spinach and garlic and cook, stirring constantly, for about 5 minutes, or until you smell the garlic cooking and the oil is absorbed. Season with salt and pepper. Set aside.

3. Using about half of the ham, cover the bottom of the baking dish with overlapping slices. Using about one-third of the cheese, cover the ham with a layer of cheese. Spread all of the spinach mixture over the cheese. Spread all of the salami over the spinach and then another layer of cheese over the salami. (You can see how this is going to be very good.) Cut the red pepper in strips about 1 inch wide and spread the strips over the cheese. Spread the remaining cheese over the peppers, then all the remaining ham in overlapping slices. Set the filling aside while you roll the crust.

Continued

4. Prepare the topping: Lightly flour the rolling surface and rolling pin. Roll the crust dough to a shape that is 1 inch larger than the top of the baking dish. Roll the crust around the rolling pin and unroll it over the top of the baking dish. Fold $1/2$ inch of the edge of the crust under to form a smooth edge. Use your thumb and forefinger to pinch the edge into a scalloped pattern or fluted edge around the edge of the dish, while pressing it firmly onto the rim. Use a pastry brush to brush the top of the dough lightly with the egg wash. Cut four 2-inch-long slits in the top of the crust to release steam while the potpie bakes.

5. Bake for about 25 minutes, or until the crust is browned and you can hear the filling bubbling gently, which signals that the cheese is melted. Remove from the oven and let rest for 10 minutes, then use a large knife to cut wedges of crust and filling. Or, let the potpie cool to room temperature for about 30 minutes and serve.

BEEF & VEGETABLE COTTAGE PIE

Makes **8** servings

COOKING THE FILLING:
ABOUT 20 MINUTES

POTPIE BAKING:
375°F FOR ABOUT
35 MINUTES

3 medium potatoes (1½ pounds), peeled and cut into 1½- to 2-inch pieces

Salt

1 pound lean ground beef

1 tablespoon corn or canola oil

1 cup coarsely chopped onion (1 medium)

½ cup finely chopped carrots (2 medium)

½ cup finely chopped celery (2 stalks)

1 large leek (white part only), halved lengthwise, cleaned, and cut into thin slices

2 cloves garlic, finely chopped

½ cup chicken broth (low sodium if canned)

2 tablespoons tomato paste

¼ cup whole milk

2 tablespoons unsalted butter, melted

Freshly ground black pepper

A Step Ahead: Assemble the cottage pie early in the day, cover it, and refrigerate it to be baked later in the day. A cold potpie will need about 5 additional minutes of baking time.

Variations: One pound of lean ground lamb can substitute for the ground beef.

Cottage pie is really two recipes in one. If made with ground beef and vegetables it is cottage pie, and if made with ground lamb it becomes shepherd's pie. The traditional (and easy) mashed potato topping is the same for both. The potatoes can be mashed quickly by beating them with an electric mixer, but a potato masher works as well.

1. Put the potatoes in a medium saucepan, fill it with enough water to cover the potatoes, and season with salt. Cover the pot and bring the water to a boil over high heat, then adjust the heat to cook the potatoes at a gentle simmer until they test tender with a fork, about 20 minutes.

2. Position a rack in the middle of the oven. Preheat the oven to 375°F. Have ready a baking dish with a 2½- to 3-quart capacity.

3. In a large skillet over medium heat, cook the ground beef until it is no longer pink, stirring with a fork to break up any clumps. Remove the meat to a large bowl and set aside. Heat the oil in the skillet for 1 minute. Reduce the heat to medium-low and add the onion, carrots, celery, leek, and garlic. Cover the pan and cook the vegetables for about 5 minutes just to soften them. Stir the vegetables into the reserved cooked meat. Put the chicken broth in a small bowl and stir in the tomato paste, then stir it into the meat mixture. Add salt and pepper. Transfer the filling to the baking dish.

4. Drain the potatoes and put them in the large bowl of an electric mixer. Add the melted butter and milk and beat on low speed until smooth, about 30 seconds. Season with salt and pepper and spread the potatoes over the filling. Use the back of a fork to draw a design of crisscrossing lines over the top.

5. Bake until the edges of the potato topping are browned and the filling is bubbling gently, about 35 minutes. Use a large spoon to scoop out servings of potato and filling.

TORTELLINI & PANCETTA POTPIE

6 ounces pancetta, cut into
1/2-inch pieces

1 tablespoon plus 1 teaspoon olive oil

1 cup finely chopped onion (1 medium)

2 large cloves garlic, finely chopped

1/4 cup lightly packed coarsely
chopped fresh basil

3/4 cup chicken broth
(low sodium, if canned)

1/3 cup heavy whipping cream

1/4 cup freshly grated Parmesan cheese

1/8 teaspoon salt

1/8 teaspoon freshly ground
black pepper

9 ounces (about 2 1/2 cups)
cheese-filled egg tortellini

9 ounces (about 2 1/2 cups)
cheese-filled spinach tortellini

Extremely Flaky Sour Cream Crust
(page 22)

Makes **6** servings

COOKING THE FILLING:
ABOUT 22 MINUTES

POTPIE BAKING:
400°F FOR ABOUT
40 MINUTES

Spinach-and-egg tortellini make a colorful filling for this pasta potpie. Toss a salad to go with it, and you have a dinner suitable for company or family.

NOTE: **Pancetta is unsmoked bacon and can be found at Italian food shops and many deli counters. Be sure to ask for it to be sliced thinly. If pancetta is not available, thinly sliced lean bacon or prosciutto can substitute.**

—————～～～～～～～～———————

1. Position a rack in the middle of the oven. Preheat the oven to 400°F. Rub 1 teaspoon olive oil inside a baking dish with an 8–cup capacity.

2. In a medium skillet, cook the pancetta pieces over medium heat until the edges brown, about 10 minutes. Transfer the pancetta to a large bowl. In the same skillet, heat the 1 tablespoon olive oil over medium heat for 1 minute. Add the onion and cook until it softens, about 5 minutes. Add the garlic and basil and cook for 1 minute. Stir in the chicken broth and adjust the heat to cook it at a gentle boil until it is reduced to about 1/2 cup, about 5 minutes. Add the cream, bring to a boil, then immediately remove the pan from the heat. Stir in the Parmesan cheese. Stir the sauce into the pancetta in the bowl. Add the salt and pepper and taste for seasoning. Set aside.

3. In a large pot of salted boiling water, cook the tortellini for 5 minutes. Drain the tortellini well and stir them into the pancetta and sauce to coat them with sauce. Transfer the pasta to the baking dish.

Continued

Crust Options: You-Can-Do-It Flaky Crust (page 19) or Surefire Cream Cheese Crust (page 21) can be used for this potpie. Or, use thawed frozen puff pastry.

4. Lightly flour the rolling surface and rolling pin. Roll the dough to a shape that is 1 inch larger than the top of the baking dish. Roll the crust around the rolling pin and unroll it over the top of the baking dish. Fold $^1/_2$ inch of the edge of the crust under to form a smooth edge. Use your thumb and forefinger to pinch the edge into a scalloped pattern or fluted edge around the edge of the dish, while pressing it firmly onto the rim. Cut four 2-inch-long slits in the top of the crust to release steam while the potpie bakes. Use a pastry brush to brush the top with the 1 teaspoon olive oil.

5. Bake for about 40 minutes, or until the crust is lightly browned. Let rest for 5 minutes, then use a large knife to cut wedges of crust and filling.

LOBSTER POTPIE

2 tablespoons unsalted butter

1/3 cup finely chopped onion

2 tablespoons unbleached all-purpose flour

1/2 cup whole milk

3/4 cup chicken broth (low sodium if canned)

2 tablespoons dry sherry

Salt and freshly ground black pepper

1 pound cooked lobster meat, cut into bite-size pieces

Extremely Flaky Sour Cream Crust (page 22)

2 teaspoons unsalted butter, melted, for brushing top

Crust Options: You-Can-Do-It Flaky Crust (page 19) or Surefire Cream Cheese Crust (page 21) can be used for these pot-pies. Or, use thawed frozen puff pastry.

Individual servings of lobster potpie are as elegant as a potpie can be. The lobster is definitely the main attraction, so a hint of sherry to flavor the light cream sauce is all the enhancement needed for the filling.

1. Position a rack in the middle of the oven. Preheat the oven to 375°F. Put 4 oven-proof baking dishes or ovenproof bowls with a 2-cup capacity on a baking sheet. The baking sheet makes it easier to move the baking dishes in and out of the oven.

2. In a medium saucepan, melt the butter over low heat. Add the onion and cook until it softens, about 5 minutes. Add the flour and increase the heat to medium. Using a wooden spoon and stirring constantly, cook until it begins to turn golden, about 2 minutes. Whisking constantly, slowly pour in the milk, chicken broth, and sherry. Bring to a gentle boil, adjusting the heat as necessary, and cook for about 3 minutes, or until the sauce thickens slightly. Remove from the heat and season with salt and pepper. Divide the lobster meat among the 4 dishes and pour about 1/3 cup sauce over each. Set aside to cool while you roll the crust.

3. Cut the dough into 4 equal pieces, one for each lobster pie. Lightly flour the rolling surface and rolling pin. Roll one piece of dough to a shape that is 3/4 inch larger than the top of the baking dish. Roll the crust around the rolling pin and unroll it over the filling. Fold 1/2 inch of the edge of the crust under to form a smooth edge. Pinch the edge into a fluted pattern around the edge while pressing it firmly onto the rim. Cut two 2-inch-long slits in the top of the crust to release steam while the potpie bakes. Repeat with the remaining 3 baking dishes. Use a pastry brush to brush the top of each crust lightly with melted butter.

4. Bake for about 20 minutes, or until the crust is lightly browned and the filling is beginning to gently bubble. Protecting your hands with pot holders, put the hot baking dishes on individual plates and serve.

SAUSAGE & MASH POTPIE WITH ROASTED ONION GRAVY

2 medium onions, halved and thinly sliced

1 tablespoon olive oil

6 pork, chicken, or turkey sausages (about 1 1/2 pounds)

3 medium potatoes (1 1/2 pounds), peeled and cut into 1 1/2- to 2-inch pieces

Salt

1 tablespoon Worcestershire sauce

1 teaspoon mustard powder

2 cups beef broth (low sodium if canned)

1 tablespoon corn or canola oil

5 teaspoons unbleached all-purpose flour

2 tablespoons red wine

2 tablespoons unsalted butter, melted

1/4 cup whole milk

Freshly ground black pepper

Whenever my husband, Jeff, and I visit London, we drop our suitcases and head straight over to Sausage and Mash on Portobello Road. We order a dish of their prize-winning sausages with roasted-onion gravy and mashed potatoes, sit down at one of the long tables, and wait for a plate of English soul food at its best.

NOTE: Traditionally, this dish calls for well-seasoned pork sausages, but spicy sausages made with chicken or turkey work just fine.

—〜〜〜〜〜〜〜—

1. Position a rack in the middle of the oven. Preheat the oven to 400°F. Have ready a baking dish with an 8-cup capacity.

2. Spread out the onions on a baking sheet. Drizzle the olive oil over the onions. Put the sausages on top of the onions. Cook, using tongs to turn the sausages, until the outside of the sausages are browned on all sides, about 25 minutes. Remove the sausages to a plate and set aside to cool slightly. Continue cooking the onions for 10 more minutes to crisp them slightly. Remove the onions from the oven. Reduce the oven temperature to 375°F. Cook the potatoes for the topping while the sausages and onions bake.

3. Put the potatoes in a medium saucepan, fill it with enough water to cover the potatoes, and sprinkle in some salt (about 1/4 teaspoon). Cover the pot and bring the water to a boil over high heat, then adjust the heat to cook the potatoes at a gentle simmer until they test tender with a fork, about 20 minutes.

Continued

Drain the potatoes and put them in the large bowl of an electric mixer.

4. In a small bowl, stir the Worcestershire, mustard powder, and beef broth together to dissolve the mustard powder. Set aside. In a medium saucepan, heat the oil over medium heat. Add the flour and stir constantly until it begins to turn a golden color, about 3 minutes. Stir in the roasted onions and wine, cooking until the wine evaporates, about 15 seconds. Add the broth mixture and adjust the heat to bring the gravy to a simmer (tiny bubbles) and cook for 5 minutes. The gravy will thicken slightly. Cut the cooled sausages into 1-inch pieces and add to the gravy. Pour the sausages and gravy into the baking dish.

5. Add the melted butter and milk to the potatoes and beat on low speed until the potatoes are smooth, about 30 seconds. Add salt to taste and a generous quantity of pepper and use a spoon to gently drop spoonfuls of the warm potatoes over the filling in the baking dish, gently spreading the potatoes as you spoon them and carefully covering the sausages and gravy. (Warm mashed potatoes spread easily.) Use a spoon to gently smooth the top.

6. Bake for about 15 minutes, or just until the potato topping is hot. The filling should not cook long enough to bubble vigorously or it will bubble up through the potato topping. Use a large spoon to scoop out servings of potato and filling.

SALMON COULIBIAC POTPIE

Makes **10** servings

COOKING THE FILLING: ABOUT 30 MINUTES

POTPIE BAKING: 400°F FOR ABOUT 35 MINUTES

2 pounds salmon fillet

1/4 cup dry white wine or dry white vermouth

1/4 medium onion, sliced

1/2 lemon, quartered

1 bay leaf

1/2 teaspoon salt

1 3/4 cup chicken broth (low sodium if canned)

3/4 cup long-grain rice

2 tablespoons unsalted butter

1/2 pound mushrooms, chopped coarsely (white or cremini preferred)

2 cups finely chopped onions (2 medium)

2 teaspoons finely grated lemon zest

2 tablespoons fresh lemon juice

1/3 cup lightly packed finely chopped fresh dill

4 hard-boiled eggs, coarsely chopped

Freshly ground black pepper

1 1/2 recipes Extremely Flaky Sour Cream Crust (page 22)

1 large egg beaten with 2 tablespoons heavy whipping cream for egg wash

1 cup sour cream mixed with 1/4 cup chopped fresh dill for serving (optional)

4 tablespoons unsalted butter, melted and mixed with 1 tablespoon fresh lemon juice and 2 teaspoons chopped fresh dill for serving (optional)

Try this Russian classic for your fanciest party. The baking dish holds a mounded filling of poached salmon, mushrooms, and hard-boiled eggs, covered with a flaky sour cream crust. Since this crust is decorated with strips of dough, the recipe calls for preparing extra dough. The seasonings of fresh dill and lemon make this a perfect choice for a spring celebration.

The filling is made by cooking the salmon in simmering water, cooking rice in chicken broth, and cooking the onion and mushrooms lightly in butter. Once this is done, all of the filling ingredients are mixed together and the filling is ready for its crust topping and baking.

---

1. Position a rack in the middle of the oven. Preheat the oven to 400°F. Have ready a 9- or 10-by-2-inch round baking dish or a 10-inch glass pie dish that is 2 inches deep.

2. Fill a nonreactive 3-quart or larger pot, preferably with an oval shape, with enough water to cover the salmon. Heat the water until it is simmering gently. You will see small bubbles. Add the wine, sliced onion, lemon, bay leaf, and 1/4 teaspoon of the salt. Carefully put the salmon in the water. Cover tightly and cook for about 15 minutes, keeping the liquid at a low simmer (tiny bubbles) until the salmon is firm to the touch and no longer soft in the center at its thickest point. The cooked fish should be an even light pink all the way through. Use a fork to flake a piece off from the center to check that it is done, if necessary. Put the fish on a platter and remove any skin and discard it. Let the salmon cool slightly, then use a fork to flake the salmon into pieces about 1/2 to 3/4 inch in size, removing any pinbones as you go. Meanwhile, cook the rice.

3. In a medium saucepan, bring the broth to a boil over medium-high heat. Add the remaining 1/2 teaspoon of salt and the rice, reduce the heat to low, cover tightly, and cook until the rice is tender, about 20 minutes. Set aside.

Continued

4. In a medium skillet, melt 1 tablespoon of the butter over medium-high heat until it just begins to bubble. Add the mushrooms and cook until they are soft and their moisture has evaporated, about 7 minutes. Remove the mushrooms to a large bowl. Heat the remaining 1 tablespoon butter, add the 2 cups chopped onions, and cook until they soften, about 5 minutes. Add them to the mushrooms in the bowl.

5. Add the flaked salmon, rice, lemon zest, lemon juice, dill, and chopped eggs to the mushrooms and onions in the bowl and stir them together. Season with pepper. Spoon the filling into the baking dish, mounding it toward the center to make a rounded hill shape.

6. Lightly flour the rolling surface and rolling pin. Take two-thirds of the crust dough (1 recipe) and roll it to a shape that is 1 inch larger than the top of the baking dish. Roll the crust around the rolling pin and unroll it over the top of the baking dish. Let it hang over the edges of the dish while you roll out the remainder of the dough for the lattice decoration. Use a pastry brush to brush the top of the dough lightly with the egg wash.

7. Roll the remaining dough ($^1/_2$ recipe) into a rectangle that measures about 5 by 12 inches. Cut 10 strips 12 inches long and $^1/_2$ inch wide. Using a long, thin metal spatula to help lift the dough, and beginning 1 inch from the edge of the baking dish, place 5 dough strips evenly over the crust. Turn the baking dish a $^1/_8$ revolution. Spacing them about $1^1/_2$ inches apart, place the remaining 5 dough strips over the crust. Trim the strips even with the outer edge of the crust. The strips will form a crisscrossing diamond pattern.

8. Fold the dough hanging over the edge of the crust toward the inside of the crust, pressing it firmly onto the edge of the baking dish to seal the dough strips under the crust and make a smooth edge. Gently brush the dough strips with the egg wash. Cut a small hole in the center of the dough to let steam escape.

9. Bake for about 35 minutes, or until the crust is lightly browned and the filling is hot. Use a large knife to cut wedges and a wide spatula or pancake turner to lift the filling with its crust from the baking dish. Pass the cold sour cream and dill sauce or the lemon butter dill sauce, or both, to spoon over the potpie, if desired.

Crust Options: 1½ recipes of Surefire Cream Cheese Crust (page 21) can be used for this potpie. Or, use a thawed frozen puff pastry.

FRENCH SPICED-BEEF HASH POTPIE WITH MASHED POTATO TOPPING

Filling

2 tablespoons unsalted butter

2 cups finely chopped onions (2 medium)

3 cloves garlic, finely chopped

2 tomatoes, peeled and coarsely chopped (see page 11)

2 tablespoons chopped fresh parsley

2 cups beef or chicken broth (low sodium if canned)

2 tablespoons unbleached all-purpose flour

1/2 pound pastrami, corned beef, or boiled beef, cut into 1/2-inch pieces (2 cups)

Salt and freshly ground black pepper

Topping

3 medium potatoes (1 1/2 pounds), peeled and cut into 1 1/2- to 2-inch pieces

Salt

2 tablespoons unsalted butter, melted

1/4 cup whole milk

2 tablespoons freshly grated Parmesan cheese

Freshly ground black pepper

1/2 cup fresh bread crumbs

If you are feeling in an *à la Française* mood, call this potpie *hachis Parmentier*. That is the French name for this dish, which is often made from spiced leftover boiled beef topped with mashed potatoes and bread crumbs. Since I seldom have leftover boiled beef (actually, never), I find that corned beef or pastrami makes an excellent substitution.

~~~~~~~~~~~~~~

1. Position a rack in the middle of the oven. Preheat the oven to 350°F. Have ready a baking dish with a 6-cup capacity.

2. Make the filling: Melt the butter in a large skillet over medium heat. Add the onions and cook them for 3 minutes. Add the garlic and continue cooking for about 5 minutes more, or until the onions soften. Add the tomatoes and parsley and cook until most of the juice from the tomatoes evaporates, about 5 minutes. Put 1/2 cup of the broth in a small bowl and stir in the flour to dissolve it. Add the broth mixture and the remaining 1 1/2 cups broth to the pan and cook, stirring often, until the sauce thickens, about 10 minutes. Adjust the heat to keep the sauce bubbling gently. When the sauce begins to thicken, add the pastrami or other meat and cook for 5 minutes. Remove from the heat and season with salt and pepper. If using pastrami or corned beef, you may not need to add salt. Transfer the filling to the baking container and set aside.

3. Make the topping: Put the potatoes in a medium saucepan, fill it with enough water to cover the potatoes, and sprinkle in some salt (about 1/4 teaspoon). Cover the pot and bring the water to a boil over high heat, then adjust the heat to cook the potatoes at a simmer (tiny bubbles) until they test tender with a fork, about 20 minutes. Drain the potatoes and put them in the large bowl of an electric mixer. Add the melted butter, milk, and Parmesan cheese and beat on low speed until the potatoes are smooth, about 30 seconds. Add salt and pepper to taste and carefully drop the mashed potatoes by the teaspoon over the filling in the baking dish. Use the back of the spoon to gently spread the potatoes to cover the filling. The filling is soft, so be careful to spread the potatoes gently so they do not sink into the filling. Sprinkle the bread crumbs over the potatoes.

4. Bake until the edges of the potato topping are browned and the filling just begins to bubble at the edges, about 35 minutes. Use a large spoon to scoop out servings of potato and filling.

NEW TAKES on POTPIES

I had fun developing these potpies. Some favorite stews, long-simmered dishes, meat loaves (ham, in this case), and basic breakfast combinations were transformed into potpies. The ideas came from my tried-and-true recipes, dishes from friends and family, and putting together ingredients that I like. Then there was the lucky day that I was inspired to make Costa Rican Spicy Picadillo & Plantain Potpie (page 80), when I spotted some plantains in my local market.

Dishes that lend themselves to becoming a potpie filling are juicy and savory, like Joe's Special, Swiss steak, or chicken cooked in red wine. A grilled steak doesn't work in a potpie, but chunks of steak simmered in red wine certainly do. After choosing a filling, the next step is to add an appropriate topping. Examples of toppings that relate to their fillings are the potatoes found in and on Quick Choucroute Potpie (page 93) or the biscuit topping for Sausage & Biscuit Potpie (page 87). Take a look at some of your dinner favorites; you may already have some "new takes" of your own.

CHICKEN in RED WINE POTPIE

Makes **8** servings

COOKING THE FILLING:
1¾ TO 2 HOURS

POTPIE BAKING:
400°F FOR ABOUT
35 MINUTES

Filling

2 tablespoons olive oil

One 3½- to 4-pound chicken, whole or cut up (remove giblets)

4 strips thick-sliced bacon, cut into 1-inch pieces

8 ounces medium to large white or cremini mushrooms (about 10), halved

2 cups coarsely chopped onions (2 medium)

2 carrots, peeled and sliced about ¼ inch thick

5 cloves garlic

2 tablespoons unbleached all-purpose flour

1 bottle dry red wine (3 cups)

Four 2- to 3-inch-long fresh thyme sprigs, or 1 teaspoon dried thyme

8 ounces (about 14) small whole onions, peeled and left whole

Salt and freshly ground black pepper

Topping

Extremely Flaky Sour Cream Crust (page 22)

1 large egg beaten with 2 tablespoons heavy whipping cream for egg wash

Whether you call it Chicken in Red Wine Potpie for the family or Coq au Vin Potpie for company, this is French home cooking at its best. The rich flavors of the wine are cooked into the chicken. The sauce starts out the color of the wine and then cooks down to a deep mahogany color.

I prefer to put a whole chicken in a large pot and let it cook in its wine bath, but a cut-up chicken also works fine. As long as you use a large 5-quart pot, the chicken can be cooked either way. Almost 2 hours may seem like a long time to cook the filling, but 1 hour is for the chicken to just bubble away by itself and 30 minutes is for the sauce to reduce and thicken slightly. Neither step needs much attention.

1. **Make the filling:** Have ready a baking dish with an 8-cup capacity. In a large (5-quart) saucepan or Dutch oven, heat 1 tablespoon of the olive oil over medium heat for 1 minute. Add the chicken and cook, using tongs to turn the chicken once, until lightly browned, about 5 minutes. The chicken is not cooked at this point, just browned on the outside. The whole chicken will not be browned in every spot. Remove the chicken to a clean plate and set aside.

2. Add the bacon pieces and cook until they begin to crisp, about 8 minutes. Remove to a clean plate and set aside. Carefully pour off all but 1 teaspoon of the bacon fat and discard it. Add the mushrooms and cook just until any moisture evaporates and they brown slightly, about 5 minutes. Remove the mushrooms to a clean plate and set aside. Heat the remaining 1 tablespoon olive oil in the saucepan and add the chopped onions, carrots, and garlic. Cook just until the onions soften, about 5 minutes, stirring often. Add the flour, stirring it to combine it with the vegetables. Stir the vegetables and flour constantly for 1 minute to cook the flour. Pour in the wine, stirring it to mix it with the vegetables. Add the thyme and bacon pieces. Return the chicken to the pot. Spoon the liquid over the chicken, cover the pot, and simmer (gently bubbling) the whole chicken for about an hour or until tender, using tongs to turn the

A Step Ahead: Make the filling 1 day ahead, let it cool for about 30 minutes, then cover and refrigerate.

Crust Options: You-Can-Do-It Flaky Crust (page 19) or Surefire Cream Cheese Crust (page 21) can be used for this potpie. Or, use a store-bought refrigerated pie crust.

chicken in the sauce several times. If using chicken pieces, they will be done in about 45 minutes. Remove the chicken to a clean plate to rest just until it is cool enough to remove from the bones and shred.

3. Add the mushrooms and onions to the sauce in the pan and cook, uncovered and at a gentle boil, for about 30 minutes until the sauce thickens slightly to a syrupy consistency and the onions are fork-tender. The sauce will reduce to about 2 cups. Adjust the heat to keep the sauce bubbling gently. Remove the sauce from the heat.

4. Cut or pull off the chicken from the bones and discard the skin. Use your clean fingers to shred the chicken meat. Stir the chicken into the thickened sauce. Season with salt and pepper. Transfer the filling to the baking dish and let it cool for about 15 minutes while you roll the crust. Or, cover the filling with plastic wrap and refrigerate it for up to 1 day.

5. Position an oven rack in the middle of the oven. Preheat the oven to 400°F.

6. Prepare the topping: Lightly flour the rolling surface and rolling pin. Roll the crust dough to a shape that is 1 inch larger than the top of the baking dish. Roll the crust around the rolling pin and unroll it over the top of the baking dish. Fold 1/2 inch of the edge of the crust under to form a smooth edge. Use your thumb and forefinger to pinch the edge into a fluted or scalloped pattern around the edge of the dish while pressing it firmly onto the rim. Cut four 2-inch-long slits in the top of the crust to release steam while the pie bakes. Use a pastry brush to brush the crust lightly with the egg wash.

7. Bake for about 35 minutes, or until the crust is lightly browned and the filling just begins to bubble gently beneath the crust. If the filling bubbles vigorously, it can bubble up through the crust. Not a disaster, but the crust will have sauce on top and not be as crisp. Serve the potpie by using a large spoon to cut down through the crust and scoop out servings of crust and filling.

GRANDMA TILLIE'S SWISS STEAK POTPIE

1½ pounds ½-inch-thick sirloin steak, cut into 6 pieces

¼ cup unbleached all-purpose flour

Salt and freshly ground black pepper

2 tablespoons canola or corn oil

1 cup coarsely chopped onion (1 medium)

½ cup coarsely chopped celery (2 stalks)

1 medium green bell pepper, seeded, deveined, and coarsely chopped

2 cups beef broth (low sodium if canned)

1 tablespoon tomato paste

You-Can-Do-It Flaky Crust (page 19)

My husband's Grandma Tillie cooked by instinct, and her instincts were always right on track. Of course, when one wanted to duplicate one of her recipes, it was never as easy as looking in her recipe file, which didn't exist. I learned how to cook her Swiss steak by sitting at the big table in her Midwestern kitchen and watching her cook. As Grandma cooked, I made notes, so now, decades later, I can make her potpie of falling-apart-tender steak in rich brown gravy and can pass it on to my children and someday Grandma Tillie's great-great-grandchildren.

Although the filling must cook for over an hour before the potpie bakes, it needs little attention while it is cooking. The filling can be cooked a day ahead; it only gets better by being refrigerated overnight and baked with its crust the following day.

———～～～～～～～———

1. Have ready a baking dish with an 8–cup capacity. Trim any fat from the edges of the meat and discard it. Use a meat pounder or mallet to pound the steak to flatten the pieces slightly. Use paper towels to pat the steak dry on both sides. Lay a large piece of waxed paper on the counter. Put the flour on a large plate and season it with a sprinkling of salt and generous grindings of black pepper, stirring to distribute the salt and pepper. Dip both sides of each piece of steak in the seasoned flour, shaking the excess flour gently back onto the plate, and arrange them in one layer on the waxed paper.

2. In a large skillet, heat the oil over medium heat for about 1 minute. Transfer the steak pieces to the skillet and cook them, turning once with tongs, to brown both sides, about 5 minutes. Cook the meat in 2 batches if necessary to avoid crowding. Remove the meat to a clean plate and set aside.

Continued

Crust Options: Surefire Cream Cheese Crust (page 21) or Extremely Flaky Sour Cream Crust (page 22) can be used for this potpie. Or, use a store-bought refrigerated pie crust.

3. Add the onion, celery, and bell pepper to the skillet and cook over medium heat, stirring often, until soft, about 7 minutes. Add the beef broth and tomato paste, stirring and scraping with a wooden spoon to loosen any brown bits. Return the steak to the pan along with any accumulated juices. Cover the pan loosely and cook on low heat, keeping the liquid at a gentle boil (a few large bubbles) until the gravy thickens slightly and the meat is fork-tender, about 1 hour. Flip the pieces of meat over once during the cooking. Taste the gravy and add salt and pepper. Transfer the filling to the baking dish, letting it cool for about 15 minutes while you roll the crust. Or, cover the slightly cooled filling with plastic wrap and refrigerate it for up to 1 day.

4. Position an oven rack in the middle of the oven. Preheat the oven to 400°F.

5. Lightly flour the rolling surface and rolling pin. Roll the crust dough to a shape that is 1 inch larger than the top of the baking dish. Roll the crust around the rolling pin and unroll it over the top of the baking dish. Fold $1/2$ inch of the edge of the crust under to form a smooth edge. Use your thumb and forefinger to pinch the edge into a scalloped pattern around the edge of the dish while pressing it firmly onto the rim. Cut four 2-inch-long slits in the top of the crust to release steam while the pie bakes.

6. Bake the potpie for about 25 minutes, or until the crust is lightly browned. Let it rest for 5 minutes, then use a large spoon to cut down through the crust and scoop out servings of crust and filling.

JOE'S SPECIAL POTPIE

2 tablespoons olive oil

2 pounds lean ground beef

2 cups coarsely chopped onions (2 medium)

1 package (10 ounces) thawed frozen chopped spinach, drained well and squeezed dry

2 cloves garlic, finely chopped

1/2 teaspoon dried oregano

1/4 teaspoon freshly grated nutmeg

1 teaspoon salt

1/2 teaspoon freshly ground black pepper

4 large eggs, lightly beaten

Extremely Flaky Sour Cream Crust (page 22)

Crust Options: You-Can-Do-It Flaky Crust (page 19) or Surefire Cream Cheese Crust (page 21) can be used for this pot-pie. Or, use thawed frozen puff pastry.

When my husband and I were newly married and living in San Francisco, one of our favorite things to do on a night out was to eat at a "Joe's." These were restaurants that specialized in simple Italian food and also served Joe's Special. This ground beef, onion, and spinach hash is seasoned with oregano and a bit of nutmeg (the secret season-ing) and then finished with eggs to bind it together. Now, as a potpie, Joe's Special can be made ahead of time, and a sour cream crust is the perfect crisp addition.

—————~~~~~~~~~—————

1. Have ready a baking dish with a 2 1/2 quart capacity. In a large skillet, heat the oil over medium-high heat for 1 minute. Add the ground beef and cook, stirring with a fork to break up any clumps, until it is no longer pink. Reduce the heat to medium, add the onions, and cook until they soften and any meat juices evaporate, about 10 minutes. Add the spinach, garlic, oregano, nutmeg, salt, and pepper and cook for about 2 minutes, stirring to mix thoroughly. Add the eggs and continue cooking and stirring until the eggs are amalgamated into the mixture and it no longer looks wet. Transfer the filling to the baking dish, letting it cool for about 15 minutes while you roll the crust. Or, cover the cooled filling with plastic wrap and refrigerate it for up to 1 day.

2. Position an oven rack in the middle of the oven. Preheat the oven to 375°F.

3. Lightly flour the rolling surface and rolling pin. Roll the crust dough to a shape that is 1 inch larger than the top of the baking dish. Roll the crust around the rolling pin and unroll it over the top of the dish. Fold 1/2 inch of the edge of the crust under to form a smooth edge. Use your thumb and forefinger to pinch a fluted edge around the dish while pressing it firmly onto the rim. Cut four 2-inch-long slits in the top of the crust to release steam while the potpie bakes.

4. Bake for about 20 minutes, or until the crust is lightly browned. Let rest for 5 minutes, then use a large spoon to cut down through the crust and scoop out servings of crust and filling.

MEDITERRANEAN FISH STEW POTPIE

Makes **10** servings

COOKING THE FILLING:
ABOUT 17 MINUTES

POTPIE BAKING:
375°F FOR ABOUT
30 MINUTES

One 28-ounce can tomatoes

3 tablespoons olive oil

2 cups coarsely chopped leeks
(2 to 3 large), including about
1 inch of green parts

2 cloves garlic, finely chopped

1½ cups coarsely chopped green
bell pepper (1 large)

2 cups thinly sliced (¼ inch thick)
celery (4 stalks)

1 teaspoon fennel seed

1 teaspoon red pepper flakes

1 teaspoon curry powder

1 teaspoon dried thyme

2 tablespoons finely chopped
fresh parsley

3 cups water

½ cup dry white wine

1½ to 2 pounds lean fish fillets, cut
into 1-inch chunks (haddock, halibut,
cod, and salmon, or a combination of
several of these)

You-Can-Do-It Flaky Crust (page 19)

Early June in Maine can be quite chilly, but it will always find me bundled up on the deck of Cod End restaurant in Tenants Harbor, eating a steaming bowl of Mediterranean seafood stew. This lobster shack's season is short, so when they close for the winter, I turn this tomato and vegetable stew into a potpie filled with chunks of fresh fish and remember summer days on the bay.

———~~~~~~~~~———

1. Have ready a baking dish with a 3½- to 4-quart capacity. Pour the juice from the tomatoes into a small bowl and set aside. Chop the tomatoes into about ¾-inch pieces. Set aside. In a large pot (about 5 quarts), heat the olive oil over medium heat for 1 minute. Add the leeks, garlic, bell pepper, and celery and cook until they soften, about 10 minutes. Add the fennel seed, red pepper flakes, curry powder, and thyme and cook, stirring constantly, for 1 minute. Add the tomatoes with their juice, the parsley, water, and wine. Increase the heat just to bring the liquid to a boil. Add the fish pieces and cook on low heat at a gentle simmer for about 5 minutes, stirring occasionally, just until the fish is opaque throughout. Cut a piece to check it.

2. Pour the stew into the baking dish and let cool for 15 minutes while you roll the crust. The stew should be at least ¾ inch below the top of the baking dish so the crust does not sit directly on it.

3. Position a rack in the middle of the oven. Preheat the oven to 375°F.

4. Lightly flour the rolling surface and rolling pin. Roll the crust dough to a shape that is 1 inch larger than the top of the baking dish. Roll the crust around the rolling pin and unroll it over the cooled filling. Fold $1/2$ inch of the edge of the crust under to form a smooth edge. Use the tines of a fork to press the dough firmly onto the rim of the baking dish. Cut four 2-inch-long slits in the top of the crust to release steam while the pie bakes.

5. Bake about 30 minutes, or until the crust is lightly browned. Use a large spoon to cut down through the crust and scoop out servings of crust and filling.

COSTA RICAN SPICY PICADILLO PLANTAIN POTPIE

2 tablespoons corn or canola oil

2 ripe plantains, peeled and halved lengthwise

1 cup coarsely chopped onion (1 medium)

1 medium green bell pepper, seeded, deveined, and coarsely chopped

2 cloves garlic, finely chopped

1 pound lean ground beef

One 14½-ounce can tomatoes

2 tablespoons raisins

½ to 1 teaspoon red pepper flakes

2 tablespoons dry white wine or dry white vermouth

½ cup pitted and halved green olives

3 tablespoons chopped fresh parsley

Salt and freshly ground black pepper

You-Can-Do-It Flaky Crust (page 19)

1 large egg beaten with 2 tablespoons heavy whipping cream for egg wash

Several years ago my son, Peter, and I spent his spring break in the rain forests of Costa Rica. Although the rain forests were chock-full of different species of plants and animals, the food kept to a few good dishes that were made with the local ingredients. Picadillo, a spicy ground beef dish, and sweet plantain were two of those staples that stamp this potpie with its Latin American character.

NOTE: Plantains look like long bananas. They are green-skinned and savory before they ripen, and black-skinned and sweet when ripe. Depending on the dish, plantains are used at all stages of ripeness. For this potpie, let the plantains ripen at room temperature until the skins are black, and I mean black, and the fruit feels soft to the touch. This could take 5 or 6 days if they were green when purchased. It is worth the wait once you taste their sweet flesh.

~~~~~~~~~~~~~~~

1. Have ready a baking dish with an 8–cup capacity. In a large skillet, prefer-ably nonstick, heat 1 tablespoon of the oil over medium heat for 1 minute. Cut the long plantain slices in half crosswise to make them easier to manage, and cook them in the oil for about 5 minutes on each side, or until they are lightly browned. Use a wide spatula to turn them and remove them from the pan. Slide the plantain slices onto a plate, then set aside to cool slightly.

2. Heat the remaining 1 tablespoon of oil in the skillet and add the onion, bell pepper, and garlic. Cook just until the onion softens, about 5 minutes, stir-ring often. Add the ground beef and cook, stirring with a fork to break up any clumps, until it is no longer pink, about 5 minutes. Add the tomatoes with their juice, the raisins, ½ teaspoon of the red pepper flakes, the wine, and olives and cook until the juices reduce to about ½ cup, about 10 minutes. Use a fork to

Continued

break up the tomatoes into approximately 1-inch pieces as they cook. Taste the picadillo and add more of the red pepper flakes, if desired. Stir in the parsley. Cut the reserved plantain into approximately 1-inch pieces and stir them into the picadillo. Season with salt and pepper.

3. Transfer the filling to the baking dish and let it cool for about 15 minutes while you roll the crust. Or, cover the cooled filling with plastic wrap and refrigerate it for up to 1 day.

4. Position an oven rack in the middle of the oven. Preheat the oven to 375°F.

5. Lightly flour the rolling surface and rolling pin. Roll the crust dough to a shape that is 1 inch larger than the top of the baking dish. Roll the crust over the rolling pin and unroll it over the top of the baking dish. Fold $1/2$ inch of the edge of the crust under to form a smooth edge. Use your thumb and forefinger to pinch the edge into a fluted or scalloped pattern around the edge of the dish while pressing it firmly onto the rim. Cut four 2-inch-long slits in the top of the crust, then four 1-inch-long slits between the 2-inch slits to make a decorative pattern and release steam while the pie bakes. Use a pastry brush to brush the crust lightly with the egg wash.

6. Bake for about 40 minutes, or until the crust is lightly browned and the filling is bubbling gently. Serve the potpie by using a large spoon to cut down through the crust and scoop out servings of crust and filling.

BREAKFAST SPECIAL POTPIES

Filling

2 tablespoons unsalted butter

2 cups diced peeled potatoes
(¼ to ½ inch)

1 cup coarsely chopped onion
(1 medium)

2 tablespoons water

1 pound bacon, cut into 1-inch pieces
and cooked until crisp

6 large eggs

1 tablespoon finely chopped
fresh parsley

Topping

1½ cups unbleached all-purpose flour

1 tablespoon sugar

¾ teaspoon baking soda

¼ teaspoon salt

1 cup buttermilk (any fat content)

2 tablespoons corn or canola oil

A Step Ahead: The potato and bacon
mixture can be put in the baking dishes,
covered with plastic wrap, and refrigerated for up to 6 hours.

Two eggs, bacon, hash brown potatoes, and toast—$4.95. Walk into any breakfast
place and you'll see that classic breakfast offering. It is all here, baked together as
individual potpies. Start with hash brown potatoes and crisp bacon, pour the eggs
over, cover with an Irish soda bread dough, and bake. Breakfast special, yes, but also
try it for brunch or a Sunday supper.

1. Position an oven rack in the middle of the oven. Preheat the oven to 400°F.
Butter 6 ovenproof baking dishes or bowls with a 2-cup capacity and put them
on a baking sheet. The baking sheet makes it easier to move them in and out of
the oven.

2. Make the filling: In a large skillet, melt the butter over medium-high heat
for 1 minute. Add the potatoes and onion and cook, stirring often, until they
are soft and the edges are just beginning to brown, about 15 minutes. Add
the water, stirring and scraping with a spoon to loosen any brown bits, and
continue cooking just until the water evaporates, about 1 minute. Scrape the
potato mixture into a medium bowl and stir in the bacon pieces, then divide
the mixture evenly among the prepared baking dishes.

3. In a small bowl, use a fork to beat the eggs and parsley together. Dividing it
evenly, pour the egg mixture into the baking dishes. Set aside while you mix the
topping.

4. Prepare the topping: In a medium bowl, stir the flour, sugar, baking soda,
and salt together. Add the buttermilk and oil and stir just until the flour is
evenly moistened. The dough will be quite sticky. Drop large spoonfuls of the
topping over the egg mixture in each baking dish, dividing it evenly. The topping may not completely cover the eggs, but will spread as it bakes.

5. Bake until the bread topping looks golden and feels firm, about 30 minutes.
The eggs underneath will be set. Put each dish on a plate and serve immediately.

HELEN'S THAI CHICKEN POTPIE

Makes **8** servings

COOKING THE FILLING:
ABOUT 45 MINUTES

POTPIE BAKING:
400°F FOR ABOUT
20 MINUTES

Filling

1 pound boneless, skinless chicken breasts, cut into 1-inch pieces

Salt and freshly ground black pepper

3 tablespoons corn or canola oil

2 medium onions, cut into 3/4-inch pieces (2 cups)

1 large red bell pepper, seeded, deveined, and cut into 1/2-inch pieces (1 generous cup)

4 ounces green beans, halved lengthwise, or haricots verts

1/2 cup water

Two 2-inch pieces lemon zest

1 cup chicken broth (low sodium if canned)

1 cup light unsweetened coconut milk

1 teaspoon peeled and grated fresh ginger root

1/4 teaspoon red curry paste

2 teaspoons cornstarch dissolved in 2 teaspoons water

4 ounces snow peas

One 15-ounce can baby corn, drained and rinsed

4 large basil leaves, shredded

Topping

6 phyllo pastry sheets (about 13 by 17 inches), thawed if previously frozen

3 tablespoons unsalted butter, melted

My friend Helen Hall is a great cook who has lived in Asia and visited there many times. When I was writing this book, Helen came to visit, so I asked her to create an Asian-inspired potpie. She used her favorite Thai chicken dish, full of colorful vegetables and including only simple ingredients that were available in our local market. The light phyllo crust topping pairs perfectly with the delicate sauce for the filling.

———————~~~~~~~~~~———————

1. Position a rack in the middle of the oven. Preheat the oven to 400°F. Have ready a baking dish with an 8-cup capacity.

2. Make the filling: Pat the chicken pieces dry with a paper towel and sprinkle them lightly with salt and pepper. In a large skillet, heat 2 tablespoons of the oil over medium-high heat for 1 minute. Add the chicken pieces, spread them in a single layer, and cook them just until they are opaque on the outside, about 8 minutes. The chicken is not fully cooked at this point. Remove the chicken to a clean plate and set aside.

3. Reduce the heat to medium, add the remaining 1 tablespoon of oil, and cook the onions, stirring often, until they begin to soften, but not brown, about 10 minutes. Add the bell pepper and green beans and cook for 3 minutes to soften them slightly. Add the water, stirring up any brown bits, and continue cooking at a simmer until the onion is quite soft, about 5 minutes. Add the lemon zest, chicken broth, coconut milk, ginger, and curry paste, stirring them to dissolve the curry paste. Stir in the cornstarch mixture, bring to a gentle boil, and cook to thicken the sauce slightly, about 1 minute. Add the chicken and cook at a simmer for about 10 minutes until the chicken is cooked through and the sauce reduces slightly. The sauce should be the consistency of heavy cream. Season with salt and pepper. Stir in the snow peas, corn, and basil and cook for about 10 minutes to blend the flavors and cook the vegetables. Transfer the filling to the baking dish.

Continued

4. Prepare the topping: Lay out the phyllo pastry sheets in a stack. Use plastic wrap to roll up and tightly rewrap any leftover phyllo and refrigerate it for up to 1 week. Using the bottom of the baking dish as a guide, use kitchen scissors to cut 6 pieces of phyllo 1 inch larger all around than the baking dish. Immediately cover the cut sheets of phyllo completely with a damp dish towel. Place 2 pieces of the phyllo pastry on top of the filling in the dish. Brush the pastry lightly with melted butter. Repeat with 2 more pieces of phyllo. Top with the remaining 2 phyllo pieces and brush the top with butter. Tuck any overhanging edges underneath to form a smooth edge that neatly covers the filling. Cut four 1-inch-long slits in the top to let steam escape.

5. Bake until the phyllo topping is golden and crisp and the filling is bubbling gently, about 20 minutes. Use a sharp knife to cut through the crisp phyllo topping and serve.

SAUSAGE & BISCUIT POTPIE

Makes **8** servings

COOKING THE FILLING: ABOUT 35 MINUTES

POTPIE BAKING: 400°F FOR ABOUT 17 MINUTES

Filling

1 1/2 pounds ground pork sausage

2 cups finely chopped onions (2 medium)

1 green bell pepper, seeded, deveined, and finely chopped

2 tablespoons fresh parsley, finely chopped

2 cloves garlic, finely chopped

One 14 1/2-ounce can tomatoes, drained and coarsely chopped

Salt and freshly ground black pepper

Topping

1 cup unbleached all-purpose flour

2 tablespoons sugar

1/2 teaspoon baking powder

1/2 teaspoon baking soda

1/4 teaspoon salt

4 tablespoons cold unsalted butter, cut into small pieces

1/2 cup buttermilk (nonfat is fine)

This classic sausage and biscuit combination makes a good brunch or Sunday supper choice. Mixing some seasonings and vegetables into the sausage meat turns the filling into a quick meat loaf. The potpie bakes twice, once for the filling and again for the topping.

1. Position a rack in the middle of the oven. Preheat the oven to 400°F. Have ready a 9-by-2-inch round baking dish or 9-inch glass pie dish.

2. **Make the filling:** In a large bowl and using a large spoon or your clean fingers, mix the sausage, onions, bell pepper, parsley, and garlic to combine them. Spread the filling evenly in the baking dish but do not pack it down. Bake for 20 minutes. Remove the pan from the oven and carefully pour off any liquid or fat and discard it. Spoon the tomatoes evenly over top. Sprinkle lightly with salt and pepper. Return the pan to the oven for 15 more minutes. Remove the pan from the oven and let cool for at least 15 minutes while you make the topping.

3. **Prepare the topping:** In a large bowl, stir the flour, sugar, baking powder, baking soda, and salt together. Add the butter pieces. Using the paddle attachment of an electric mixer on low speed, a pastry blender, or your fingertips, mix the ingredients together until coarse crumbs form, about 1/2 to 3/4 inch in size. Add the buttermilk and continue stirring just until a soft dough forms. Gather the dough into a ball. Lightly flour the rolling surface and rolling pin and roll the dough into a 9-inch circle (about 3/4 inch thick) that fits snugly into the baking dish. Use a metal spatula to loosen the dough from the rolling surface and place it over the filling. If the dough breaks during the transfer, just pinch it together.

4. Bake until the top is evenly golden, about 17 minutes. Cut into wedges and use a wide spatula or pancake turner to lift the filling with its topping from the baking dish.

COMFORT-ME-with-EGGS POTPIE

Makes **8** servings

COOKING THE FILLING: ABOUT 16 MINUTES

POTPIE BAKING: 375°F. FOR ABOUT 25 MINUTES

Filling

8 large eggs

2 cups milk (any fat content)

1/4 cup chicken broth
(low sodium, if canned)

3 tablespoons unsalted butter

1 tablespoon grated onion

3 tablespoons unbleached
all-purpose flour

1 tablespoon Dijon mustard

1 teaspoon salt

Freshly ground black pepper

Topping

1 1/4 cups panko
(Japanese bread crumbs)

2 teaspoons paprika
(sweet Hungarian preferred)

1 tablespoon chicken broth

4 tablespoons unsalted butter, melted

1/4 teaspoon salt

Several years ago, after I had spent a long day teaching classes at Overbey's Emporium in Columbus, Ohio, the Overbeys invited me for a "rejuvenating" dinner. It turned out to be hard-boiled eggs in a creamy sauce and was the most soothing dish that I have ever eaten. The hard-boiled eggs cook in a white sauce that is lightly seasoned with mustard (to add a bit of zip), and the potpie has a crisp, golden panko topping. It is guaranteed to comfort and restore.

———~~~~~~~~———

1. Position a rack in the middle of the oven. Preheat the oven to 375°F. Have ready a 6-cup baking dish.

2. Make the filling: Put the eggs in a medium saucepan and cover with water by at least 1 inch. Bring the water to a gentle boil (just a few bubbles) and adjust the heat down from high as soon as the water begins to boil. Cook for 10 minutes, remove the pan from the heat, and let the eggs sit in the hot water for 15 minutes. Run cold water over the eggs, then peel them. Cut the eggs in half and put them in the baking dish. It is okay if there is more than one layer and they sit on top of each other. At this stage, the eggs can be covered and refrigerated overnight.

3. In a medium saucepan, heat the milk and broth over medium-low heat just until the mixture is hot and steam starts to rise from it. Do not boil. Set aside. In a medium saucepan, melt the butter with the grated onion over medium heat. Cook just until the onion softens, about 2 minutes. Stir in the flour and cook just until it begins to bubble gently, about 2 minutes. Remove the pan from the heat. Slowly pour in the hot milk mixture while whisking constantly. Return the pan to the heat and adjust the heat to cook the sauce at a gentle boil until it thickens, about 2 minutes. Remove from the heat, stir in the mustard, salt, and pepper, and taste for seasoning. Pour the sauce over the eggs in the baking dish.

4. Prepare the topping: In a medium bowl, stir the panko, paprika, chicken broth, melted butter, and salt together to evenly moisten the crumbs. Spoon the crumbs over the filling. Pat the crumbs gently to form a firm, even coating over the filling.

5. Bake until the topping is dark golden and the filling is bubbling gently, about 25 minutes.

6. Use a large spoon to cut down through the topping and scoop out servings of topping and filling.

HUNGARIAN CHICKEN GOULASH POTPIE WITH CRISP NOODLE TOPPING

Makes 8 servi

COOKING THE FILLING:
ABOUT 35 MINUTES

POTPIE BAKING:
375°F FOR ABOUT
35 MINUTES

Filling

1/2 cup unbleached all-purpose flour

Salt and freshly ground black pepper

3 boneless, skinless chicken breasts, cut into 1-inch strips

3 tablespoons corn or canola oil

4 cups thinly sliced onions (4 medium)

3 cloves garlic, finely chopped

1 teaspoon dried oregano

3 tablespoons sweet Hungarian paprika

2 1/2 cups chicken broth (low sodium if canned)

1 tablespoon tomato paste

Topping

9 ounces medium-width egg noodles

1 tablespoon oil

Salt and freshly ground black pepper

We were lucky enough to know the Sellingers, who founded the renowned Éclair bakery and café in New York City. One afternoon, after a lunch of Hungarian goulash, Mrs. Sellinger shared her goulash wisdom. She told me that using sweet Hungarian paprika and equal amounts of onions and meat were the key to making a good goulash. Simple enough, and it proved to be the goulash guide to follow.

NOTE: When working with raw chicken, be careful to prevent any contamination (see page 12). Clean all utensils and cutting areas that the chicken comes in contact with before letting any other food touch them. I cut the chicken and flour it on plates or a washable cutting board, then put the plates or cutting board and all of the utensils in the dishwasher.

1. Position a rack in the middle of the oven. Preheat the oven to 375°F. Have ready a baking dish with an 8-cup capacity.

2. **Make the filling:** Put the flour on a large plate and season it generously with salt (about 1/2 teaspoon) and pepper. Use paper towels to pat the chicken pieces dry. Dip the chicken pieces in the flour and shake off any excess. Spread the chicken on a clean plate and set aside. You will have leftover flour.

3. In a large skillet, heat 1 tablespoon of the oil over medium-high heat. Add the onions and cook until they soften, about 10 minutes, stirring often. Remove the onions to a clean plate and set aside. Heat the remaining 2 tablespoons oil in the skillet over medium-high heat. Cook the chicken pieces until they are lightly browned, about 6 minutes, turning the chicken with tongs to brown it evenly. Reduce the heat to medium and return the onions to the pan. Add

Continued

the garlic and oregano and cook for about 2 minutes, stirring constantly. Add the paprika and cook for about 1 minute, just until you smell paprika. Add the chicken broth and tomato paste and stir to dissolve the tomato paste. Cook, uncovered, for about 15 minutes, adjusting the heat to keep the sauce bubbling gently, until the chicken is opaque throughout and the sauce thickens slightly. Transfer the filling to the baking container.

4. Prepare the topping: Bring 3 quarts water to a boil in a large pot. Add a sprinkling of salt and the egg noodles. Cook the noodles for about 7 minutes, or until they are tender. Drain the noodles, put them in a large bowl, add the oil, and stir them together. Season with salt and pepper. Use a spoon to spread the noodles evenly over the filling.

5. Bake for about 35 minutes, or until the noodles are lightly browned on top. Use a large spoon to scoop out servings of noodles and filling.

QUICK CHOUCROUTE POTPIE

Filling

4 juniper berries, or a splash of gin

2 bay leaves

10 black peppercorns

2 tablespoons goose, duck, or chicken fat, or corn or canola oil

1 smoked chicken breast, or 2 smoked chicken thighs

4 chicken thighs

2 cups coarsely chopped onions (2 medium)

4 cloves garlic, finely chopped

1/2 cup dry white wine

1 pound (about 4 cups) fresh sauerkraut, drained

4 cups chopped cabbage

3/4 pound potatoes (2 medium-small), peeled and cut into 1-inch pieces

1 ham steak or 2 smoked pork chops

1 piece duck confit (leg and thigh), optional

6 mild sausages, such as knockwurst, bratwurst, or good hot dogs

6 spicy sausages, such as kielbasa or chorizo

Topping

1 pound potatoes (3 medium-small), peeled and cut into 1/4-inch-thick slices

1 tablespoon goose, duck, or chicken fat, or corn or canola oil

1/2 cup chicken broth (low sodium if canned)

"Come for quick choucroute," invited my friend Karen Good. We would never turn that invitation down. As soon as I saw the crisp sliced potato topping that covered the big pot of sausages, chicken, smoked meats, and sauerkraut, I realized that this version of choucroute was actually a potpie. The dish is quick to put together and has a long, slow baking time, so the sauerkraut and meats can soak up the flavors of each.

This wasn't a dish that Karen had ever measured, but she set about writing the recipe for me while emphasizing that the ingredients and the yield are very flexible. Her recipe said that there should be two kinds of sausages, one spicy and one on the milder side, some poultry, and some smoked meats. The spicy sausage can be chorizo or kielbasa, and the mild knockwurst, bratwurst, or even both. For the poultry, try a piece of smoked chicken and several chicken thighs and a piece of duck confit (if available) or cooked duck breast. Ham steak, smoked pork chops, or even a ham hock make good smoked-meat choices. If you want to stretch the dish to make more servings, add additional sausages or pieces of chicken. The idea is to include a variety of meats and be flexible. I cut up the sausages and meats before I serve the dish to make tasting-size portions of all of the meats. Karen says, "You can rush this, make it faster, slower, easier, or with fewer ingredients. It tastes good, regardless."

NOTE: Choose sauerkraut that comes in jars in the refrigerated section of supermarkets, or fresh sauerkraut from a local deli. Canned sauerkraut is softer and does not work as well or taste as good. Even better, order a tub of barrel-cured sauerkraut from Morse's Sauerkraut in Waldoboro, Maine (see Sources, page 130).

1. Position an oven rack on the bottom shelf of the oven. Preheat the oven to 450°F. Have ready a 5-quart or larger nonreactive pot with a cover. A Dutch oven or stainless-steel wok works well.

2. **Make the filling:** Make a seasoning packet by cutting a 6-inch square of cheesecloth, putting the juniper berries (if using), bay leaves, and peppercorns in the center, and tying it with a piece of kitchen string. Set aside.

Continued

3. In a 5-quart or larger pot, heat 1 tablespoon of the fat or oil over medium heat. Add the smoked chicken and chicken thighs and cook, using tongs to turn once to lightly brown both sides (especially the skin side, so it is crisp), about 6 minutes. Transfer the chicken to a plate and set aside. Add the remaining 1 tablespoon fat or oil and the onions and garlic. Cook for about 10 minutes, stirring often, until the onions soften. Add the wine and gin (if using), stirring and scraping with a wooden spoon to loosen any brown bits. Add the sauerkraut, cabbage, and seasoning packet. Add the potato pieces and all of the meats, arranging the sausages on top. Cover tightly and bake for 30 minutes. The cabbage will shrink. Uncover and bake for another 30 minutes. The sausages will brown nicely.

4. Prepare the topping: Reduce the oven temperature to 375°F. Carefully remove the pot from the oven. Use a large spoon to stir and distribute the meats and vegetables evenly. Press the top gently to flatten it evenly. Arrange the sliced potatoes in overlapping circular rows to cover the filling completely. You will have a pattern of 2 circular rows of potatoes. Brush the top with the fat or oil and chicken broth, being careful not to disturb the potatoes.

5. Bake, uncovered, for 1 hour, or until the potato topping is tender. The cabbage and sauerkraut will shrink considerably, and the ingredients will almost "melt" together.

6. Remove the pot from the oven. Protecting your hands (with pot holders) and the table from the hot pot, bring the pot to the table and let everyone help themselves to a selection of meats with filling and topping.

RUTH PERRY'S HAM LOAF POTPIE

Makes **6** servings

COOKING THE FILLING:
350°F FOR ABOUT
20 MINUTES PLUS
35 MINUTES

COOKING THE GLAZE:
ABOUT 5 MINUTES

POTPIE BAKING:
350°F FOR ABOUT
17 MINUTES

Filling

½ pound lean baked ham,
cut into 4 pieces

½ pound lean ground pork

¾ cup club soda or sparkling water

1 large egg

Glaze

1 cup packed dark brown sugar

1 tablespoon distilled white vinegar

2 teaspoons yellow mustard

Crust

½ cup unbleached all-purpose flour

1 tablespoon packed dark brown sugar

¼ teaspoon baking powder

¼ teaspoon baking soda

⅛ teaspoon salt

2 tablespoons cold unsalted butter,
cut into small pieces

1 cup (4 ounces) shredded sharp
Cheddar cheese

¼ cup buttermilk (nonfat is fine)

I was never lucky enough to meet Ruth Perry, but I feel that I know her well from her ham loaf potpie. Where I live in Camden, Maine, this recipe is an institution all over town, for meals from potluck dinners to fancy luncheons. After the first taste of the ham filling, saturated with a dark brown-sugar glaze and topped with a Cheddar biscuit crust, you too will know why Camden families have passed this dish down from generation to generation. The ham adds so much seasoning that it is not even necessary to add salt.

1. Position an oven rack in the middle of the oven. Preheat the oven to 350°F. Have ready a loaf pan or baking dish with a 6-cup capacity. A 9-by-5-by-3-inch loaf pan works well. Measure the inside of the top of the baking dish. The dough for the topping will be rolled to this size.

2. Make the filling: Put the ham in a food processor and pulse until it is finely ground, about 20 seconds. In a large bowl, stir the ground ham, pork, club soda, and egg together to combine them. Spoon the ham mixture into the baking container and smooth the top but do not pack it down. Bake for 20 minutes. Meanwhile, make the glaze.

3. Cook the glaze: In a small saucepan over medium-high heat, stir the brown sugar, vinegar, and mustard together and bring to a boil, stirring constantly. Remove the pan from the heat. Remove the loaf pan from the oven and pour the glaze over the filling. Return the pan to the oven and continue baking for about 35 minutes, or until the glaze is dark brown and bubbling up the sides of the pan. Remove the pan from the oven and let cool for about 15 minutes while you make the crust.

4. Make the crust: In a large bowl, stir the flour, brown sugar, baking powder, baking soda, and salt together. Add the butter pieces. Using the paddle attachment of an electric mixer on low speed, a pastry blender, or your fingertips, mix the ingredients together until coarse crumbs form, about $1/2$ to $3/4$ inch in size. Stir in the shredded cheese. Add the buttermilk and continue stirring just until a soft dough forms. Gather the dough into a ball. Lightly flour the rolling surface and rolling pin and roll the dough into a shape that will fit snugly on top of the ham loaf inside the baking dish. Use a metal spatula to loosen the dough from the rolling surface and place it on top of the ham filling. If the dough breaks during the transfer, just pinch it together.

5. Bake until the top is evenly golden, about 17 minutes. Use a large spoon to slice the loaf and to lift the ham loaf with its topping from the baking dish. The soft crust cuts easily with a spoon. The sides of the ham loaf will be glazed with the brown sugar topping.

BASQUE CHICKEN PIPÉRADE POTPIE

Makes **6** servings

COOKING THE FILLING: ABOUT 35 MINUTES

POTPIE BAKING: 375°F FOR ABOUT 25 MINUTES

1/4 cup unbleached all-purpose flour

Salt and freshly ground black pepper

1 pound (2 large) boneless, skinless chicken breasts, cut into 1-inch pieces

3 tablespoons olive oil

1 cup coarsely chopped onion (1 medium)

2 cloves garlic, finely chopped

1 medium green bell pepper, seeded, deveined, and thinly sliced

1 medium red bell pepper, seeded, deveined, and thinly sliced

1/4 cup dry white wine or dry white vermouth

One 14 1/2-ounce can tomatoes with juice, or 1 pound tomatoes, peeled and coarsely chopped (see page 11)

1/2 cup chicken broth (low sodium if canned)

3/4 teaspoon dried thyme

You-Can-Do-It Flaky Crust (page 19)

Tomatoes, bell peppers, and olive oil make the traditional good beginning for pipérade, a dish from the Basque region of southwest France. Quickly cooked chicken is the meat choice here, but other possibilities to include with a pipérade are pork, ham, other vegetables, or even scrambled eggs.

———∿∿∿∿∿∿∿∿———

1. Have ready a baking dish with an 8–cup capacity. Sprinkle the flour, a little salt, and generous grindings of black pepper onto a large plate and stir them together. Dip the chicken pieces in the seasoned flour, shaking the excess flour gently back onto the plate.

2. In a large skillet, heat 2 tablespoons of the oil over medium heat for 1 minute. Add the chicken pieces and cook them just to brown both sides, about 8 minutes. Cook the chicken in 2 batches if necessary to avoid crowding. (The chicken is not fully cooked at this point.) Remove the chicken to a clean plate and set aside.

3. Heat the remaining 1 tablespoon olive oil in the pan and add the onion, garlic, and bell peppers. Cook just to soften them, about 5 minutes, stirring often. Add the wine and cook for 1 minute until most of it evaporates. Add the tomatoes, if canned, with their juice, and if fresh with any accumulated juice, and use a fork to break them up into pieces. Add the chicken broth and thyme, stirring and scraping with a wooden spoon to loosen any brown bits. Return the chicken to the pan along with any accumulated juices. Cover the pan loosely and cook on low heat, keeping the liquid at a gentle simmer until the sauce thickens slightly and the chicken is opaque throughout, about 20 minutes. Taste the sauce and season with salt and pepper. Transfer the filling to the baking dish and let it cool for about 15 minutes while you roll the crust.

4. Position an oven rack in the middle of the oven. Preheat the oven to 375°F.

5. Lightly flour the rolling surface and rolling pin. Roll the crust dough to a shape that is 1 inch larger than the top of the baking dish. Roll the crust around the rolling pin and unroll it over the top of the baking dish. Fold $1/2$ inch of the edge of the crust under to form a smooth edge. Use your thumb and forefinger to pinch the edge into a scalloped pattern around the edge of the dish while pressing it firmly onto the rim. Cut four 2-inch-long slits in the top of the crust to release steam while the pie bakes.

6. Bake for about 25 minutes, or until the crust is lightly browned. Let rest for 5 minutes, then use a large spoon to cut down through the crust and scoop out servings of crust, sauce, and chicken.

A GARDEN of VEGETABLE POTPIES for EVERY SEASON

My vegetable potpie year begins with spring and follows the seasons. The first green onions ease one out of winter and get things started with an onion and potato potpie. Early spinach, combined with cheeses, opens another entrance to spring. Summer's rich harvest fills potpies with eggplants, tomatoes, and zucchini. Fall leeks bubble in a cream and mustard filling, and a rich Hungarian vegetable soup will warm the coldest of winter days until spring returns.

Many of these vegetable potpies can serve as hearty side dishes or light dinners. Spinach, Ricotta & Parmesan Potpie can play either role. For a vegetable potpie dinner, try Eggplant Parmesan Potpie (page 107) or Black Bean Chili Potpie with Onion and Pepper Corn Bread Topping (page 122).

When choosing vegetables, buy what is in season. They will be the freshest and in the best condition and often the least expensive. For a good part of the year, local farmers' markets or farm stands feature fresh produce that has been grown nearby. Even the smallest home garden plot, or several large pots, can hold a few tomato plants and a variety of fresh herbs. Picking from your own patch is always the freshest and most convenient choice.

ROASTED TOMATO, ONION & POTATO POTPIE WITH A PARMESAN CRUST

Makes **8** servings

COOKING THE FILLING:
20 MINUTES PLUS
35 MINUTES

POTPIE BAKING:
375°F FOR ABOUT
30 MINUTES

Crust

1¼ cups unbleached all-purpose flour

¼ teaspoon salt

½ cup (2 ounces) freshly grated Parmesan cheese

4 tablespoons cold unsalted butter, cut into pieces

3 tablespoons cold vegetable shortening, such as Crisco

4 tablespoons ice water

Filling

2 pounds ripe tomatoes (about 5 medium), peeled (page 11) and quartered

3 medium onions, halved and thinly sliced

1 pound unpeeled medium potatoes

3 tablespoons olive oil

Salt and freshly ground black pepper

¼ cup water

¾ cup (3 ounces) freshly grated Parmesan cheese

¾ teaspoon dried oregano

A side dish or main dish, good hot or at room temperature, this is a go-anywhere potpie that can travel to a picnic or potluck party or stay at home for a light supper. Roasting the vegetables is an easy way to cook them slightly crisp and to bring out their sweet flavor. Try to make this potpie when red, ripe summer tomatoes are at their best. Boiling the potatoes for about 20 minutes partially cooks them and makes them easy to peel.

———〰〰〰〰〰〰———

1. Make the crust: In the large bowl of an electric mixer on low speed, mix the flour, salt, and Parmesan cheese together for a few seconds. Stop the mixer, add the butter and shortening, then continue mixing just until the butter and shortening pieces are the size of small lima beans, about 20 seconds. With the machine running, slowly add the water 1 tablespoon at a time until the mixture begins to hold together, about 20 seconds. The dough will form large clumps and pull away from the sides of the bowl, but will not form a ball. It is fine to stop the mixer at any time and squeeze a small piece of dough to check to see if it holds together.

2. Form the dough into a disk about 6 inches in diameter. It will be easier to roll neatly if the edges are smooth, but don't handle it a lot. Wrap the dough in plastic wrap and refrigerate for at least 30 minutes or as long as overnight.

3. Position a rack in the middle of the oven. Preheat the oven to 425°F. Line a rimmed baking sheet (jelly roll pan) or a shallow roasting pan with a double layer of parchment paper for roasting the vegetables. Have ready a 9-by-2-inch round or oval baking dish or glass pie dish for baking the potpie.

4. Make the filling: Put the tomatoes and onions on the parchment-lined baking pan. Put the potatoes in a medium saucepan and fill it with enough water to cover the potatoes. Loosely cover the pot and cook the potatoes for 20 minutes. The outside (about $1/2$ inch) will be soft and the inside still firm. Put a colander in the sink and carefully pour the partially cooked potatoes into it, draining off the water. Run cold water over the potatoes until they are cool enough to handle. Use a small knife to help slip the skins off the potatoes. Cut the potatoes into 1-inch pieces and add them to the baking pan. Pour 2 tablespoons of the olive oil over the vegetables, stirring them gently to coat them evenly. Sprinkle lightly with salt and pepper. Bake until the edges of the vegetables darken and look crisp, about 35 minutes, stirring once. Set aside to cool slightly.

5. Reduce the oven temperature to 375°F. Put the roasted vegetables in the baking dish. Pour the $1/4$ cup water into the roasting pan and gently scrape up the brown bits, being careful not to tear the paper. Pour the liquid over the vegetables. Add the Parmesan cheese and oregano and stir to mix in the cheese and spread the vegetable mixture evenly in the baking dish. Taste for salt and pepper, then drizzle the remaining 1 tablespoon olive oil over the top. Let the filling cool for about 15 minutes while you roll the crust.

6. Remove the dough from the refrigerator. If it is cold and firm, let it sit at room temperature until it rolls easily. Lightly flour the rolling surface and rolling pin. Roll the dough into a shape that is 1 inch larger than the top of the baking dish. Roll the crust around the rolling pin and unroll it over the slightly cooled filling. Fold $1/2$ inch of the edge of the crust under to form a smooth edge. Use your thumb and forefinger to pinch the edge into a fluted or scalloped pattern around the edge of the dish while pressing it firmly onto the rim. Cut four 2-inch-long slits in the top of the crust to release steam while the pie bakes.

7. Bake for about 30 minutes, or until the crust is lightly browned. You will see nicely browned flecks of Parmesan cheese in the baked crust. Let rest for 5 minutes, then use a large spoon to cut down through the crust and scoop out servings of crust and filling. Or, serve at room temperature.

Steps Ahead: The tomatoes and onions can be roasted a day ahead, covered, and refrigerated overnight. The potpie can be baked in the morning or several hours ahead and reheated or served at room temperature later in the day. To reheat the potpie, bake it in a preheated 300°F oven for about 15 minutes, or until it is hot.

Variations: Four ounces of cooked bacon torn into 1-inch pieces or thinly sliced ham cut into pieces can be stirred into the roasted vegetables in the baking dish.

SPRINGTIME VEGETABLE POTPIE

Makes 6 Se

COOKING THE FILLING: ABOUT 15 MINUTES

POTPIE BAKING: 375°F FOR ABOUT 35 MINUTES

Sauce

2 tablespoons unsalted butter

2 tablespoons unbleached all-purpose flour

2 cups vegetable broth

Filling

1 tablespoon unsalted butter

2 medium onions; 1 halved and thinly sliced, and 1 coarsely chopped

2 cloves garlic, finely chopped

1/2 pound new or red-skinned potatoes, peeled and cut into 1/2-inch pieces

2 carrots, thinly sliced crosswise

2 ounces green beans (a handful), cut into 1-inch pieces

One 9-ounce package thawed frozen artichoke hearts

2 cups thawed frozen green peas

1 teaspoon finely grated lemon zest

2 tablespoons fresh lemon juice

2 tablespoons finely chopped fresh parsley

3 tablespoons finely chopped fresh dill

Salt and freshly ground black pepper

Surefire Cream Cheese Crust (page 21)

Salt and freshly ground black pepper

Bring on the tastes of spring. It's time for artichokes, peas, green beans, and new potatoes, and the fresh dill, parsley, and lemon to season them all. The sauce here has a light vegetable broth base, and the topping is a tender cream cheese crust. Frozen artichoke hearts let you put a bit of "spring" in your potpies almost any time of year.

NOTE: Canned vegetable broth is available in the supermarket in the soup section, but low-sodium chicken broth can be substituted.

———~~~~~~~~———

1. Position a rack in the middle of the oven. Preheat the oven to 375°F. Have ready a baking dish with an 8-cup capacity.

2. **Make the sauce:** In a medium saucepan, melt the butter over low heat. As soon as the butter melts, add the flour and increase the heat to medium. Using a wooden spoon and stirring constantly, cook the butter and flour until it is bubbling and it is just beginning to become slightly golden, about 1 minute. Using a whisk and whisking constantly, slowly pour in the vegetable broth. Keep whisking until the sauce is smooth. Bring to a gentle boil, adjusting the heat as necessary, and cook for 5 minutes. The sauce will thicken slightly to the consistency of a thick syrup. Set aside while you cook the onions.

3. **Make the filling:** In a large skillet, melt the butter over medium heat. Add the sliced and chopped onion and garlic and cook until the onions soften, about 5 minutes, stirring often. Add the onion mixture to the pan with the sauce. Stir in the potatoes, carrots, green beans, artichoke hearts, peas, lemon zest, lemon juice, parsley, and dill. Return the saucepan to medium heat and cook for about 10 minutes, adjusting the heat to keep the liquid at a gentle boil until the potatoes and carrots are soft, stirring often. Remove the saucepan from the heat and taste for salt and pepper. Transfer the filling to the baking dish, letting it cool for about 15 minutes while you roll the crust.

Continued

4. Lightly flour the rolling surface and rolling pin. Roll the crust dough to a shape that is 1 inch larger than the top of the baking dish. Roll the crust around the rolling pin and unroll it over the top of the baking dish. Fold $1/2$ inch of the edge of the crust under to form a smooth edge. Use your thumb and forefinger to pinch the edge into a fluted or scalloped pattern around the edge of the dish while pressing it firmly onto the rim. Use a pastry brush to brush the top lightly with water, then sprinkle lightly with salt and pepper. Cut four 2-inch-long slits in the top of the crust to release steam while the potpie bakes.

5. Bake for about 35 minutes, or until the crust is lightly browned. Let rest for 5 minutes, then use a large spoon to cut through the crust and scoop out servings of crust and filling.

EGGPLANT PARMESAN POTPIE

Makes **10** servings

COOKING THE FILLING:
25 MINUTES

POTPIE BAKING:
350°F FOR ABOUT
30 MINUTES

Tomato Sauce

2 tablespoons olive oil

2 cloves garlic, chopped

One 28-ounce can whole tomatoes

12 large fresh basil leaves,
torn into small pieces

Salt

Filling

1¹⁄₂ pounds eggplant
(3 small about 6 by 2 inches each)

¹⁄₂ cup unbleached all-purpose flour

Salt and freshly ground black pepper

2 tablespoons olive oil

Corn or canola oil for frying

2 cups Tomato Sauce (recipe above)

8 ounces fresh mozzarella cheese,
cut into ¹⁄₈-inch-thick slices

³⁄₄ cup (3 ounces) freshly grated
Parmesan cheese

Topping

1¹⁄₂ cups fresh coarse bread crumbs

³⁄₄ cup freshly grated Parmesan cheese

Salt and freshly ground black pepper

2 tablespoons water

¹⁄₄ cup olive oil

To salt or not to salt, that is the eggplant question. I salt. Salting draws out any bitterness from eggplants, and has the advantage of drawing out some of this vegetable's abundant moisture. Dipping the eggplant slices in flour before frying them cuts down on the amount of oil that they absorb (eggplant loves to absorb oil) and makes them crisp.

NOTE: The crumb topping is best when made with homemade coarse bread crumbs. When I have some bread that is becoming stale, I grind it into crumbs in the food processor, seal it tightly in a plastic freezer bag, and freeze it for up to 2 months. This quick tomato sauce was adapted from the marinara sauce recipe in Michele Scicolone's *1000 Italian Recipes*. Michele has the talent of simplifying any recipe.

———~~~~~~~~———

1. **Make the tomato sauce:** In a large skillet, heat the olive oil over medium heat for 1 minute. Add the garlic and cook just until it starts to sizzle, about 1 minute. Do not let the garlic brown. Add the tomatoes with their juice and use a fork to break them up into pieces ¹⁄₂ to ³⁄₄ inch in size. Adjust the heat so the tomato juices are bubbling gently and cook, uncovered, for 15 minutes, stirring occasionally. Add the basil and cook another 5 minutes. The sauce will reduce slightly.

2. Remove the pan from the heat, season with salt, and set aside. The sauce can be made ahead, cooled, sealed in a container, and stored in the refrigerator for up to 3 days.

3. **Make the filling:** Trim off the stems and base of the eggplants and cut them into ¹⁄₂-inch crosswise slices. Layer the slices in a colander, sprinkling each layer generously with salt. Top with a plate, then a weight (a large unopened can works well), and let sit for at least 20 minutes. You will see moisture form on the eggplant slices. Rinse off the salt and use paper towels to pat the slices dry.

4. Position a rack in the middle of the oven. Preheat the oven to 350°F. Have ready a 9-by-13-by-2-inch rectangular or oval baking dish.

Continued

5. Lay a large piece of waxed paper on the counter. Line a baking sheet with several layers of paper towels and set aside. Put the flour on a large plate and season it with a sprinkling of salt and generous grindings of black pepper, stirring to distribute the salt and pepper. Dip both sides of each eggplant slice in the seasoned flour, shaking the excess flour gently back onto the plate, and arrange them in one layer on the waxed paper. In a large skillet, combine the 2 tablespoons of olive oil with enough corn or canola oil to reach a depth of $1/4$ inch. Heat the oil over medium heat for about 3 minutes, until a slice of eggplant sizzles and bubbles gently around the edges when added. Fry a single layer of eggplant slices, turning once, until golden, about 2 minutes on each side. Use a fork or tongs to turn and lift the slices. You will probably need to fry them in 2 or 3 batches, depending on the size of the pan. Drain the slices in a single layer on the paper towel–lined baking sheet.

6. Spread $1/2$ cup of the tomato sauce over the bottom of the baking dish. Cover the bottom with half of the eggplant slices. Top with half of the mozzarella, 1 cup of the tomato sauce, and $1/4$ cup of the Parmesan cheese. Add another layer of the remaining eggplant slices, mozzarella, and sauce. Sprinkle the remaining $1/2$ cup of Parmesan cheese over the top. Set aside.

7. Prepare the topping: In a medium bowl, stir the bread crumbs and Parmesan cheese together. Stir in a sprinkling of salt and a few grindings of pepper. Stir in the water. Stir in the olive oil until the crumbs are evenly moistened and cling together. Spoon the crumbs evenly over the filling and pat them gently to smooth the top. The crumbs should completely cover the filling.

8. Bake until the topping is lightly browned and crisp and the filling is bubbling gently, about 30 minutes. Use a large, sharp knife to cut through the layers to the bottom of the dish and cut the filling into squares. Use a wide spatula or large spoon to lift the pieces onto serving plates.

A Step Ahead: The potpie can be assembled early in the day or even the day before it is baked. Cover it and store in the refrigerator. A cold potpie will need to bake an additional 5 minutes or so.

SUMMER TOMATO, CHEESE & BLACK OLIVE POTPIE

COOKING THE FILLING:
425°F FOR ABOUT
1 HOUR

POTPIE BAKING:
400°F FOR ABOUT
45 MINUTES

4 pounds tomatoes
(about 10 medium), peeled (page 11)
and halved horizontally

1/4 teaspoon salt

3 cloves garlic, finely chopped

35 fresh basil leaves, plus 2 tablespoons
tightly packed torn fresh basil leaves

3 tablespoons olive oil

1/2 cup (2 ounces) freshly grated
Parmesan cheese (Parmigiano-
Reggiano preferred)

4 ounces fresh mozzarella cheese,
cut into 1/2-inch pieces

Freshly ground black pepper

30 black olives, pitted and halved
(oil-cured olives preferred)

You-Can-Do-It Flaky Crust (page 19)

2 tablespoons heavy whipping cream
beaten with 1 large egg for egg wash

Celebrate summer with a potpie. Basil, the herb of summer, and sun-loving tomatoes bake with mozzarella and Parmesan cheese for a potpie that goes comfortably from patio to picnic. The tomatoes taste as if they have been sugared and candied, but it is just the result of roasting them. Four pounds may seem like a lot of tomatoes, but they shrink quite a bit while in the oven.

⸻⸻⁓⁓⁓⁓⁓⸻⸻

1. Have ready a 9-by-2-inch round baking dish or glass pie dish, or an oval baking dish about 11 inches long and 2 inches deep. Position a rack in the middle of the oven. Preheat the oven to 425°F.

2. Line a shallow roasting pan or rimmed baking sheet with 2 layers of parchment paper. Put the tomato halves, cut-side up, in the pan and sprinkle them with the salt and garlic. Cover each tomato with 1 or 2 of the basil leaves. Use a small spoon to drizzle 2 tablespoons of the olive oil over the basil leaves. Bake until the edges of the tomatoes begin to blacken and most or all of their moisture evaporates, about 1 hour. The basil leaves will turn dark and crisp, but they will not be burnt. Remove the tomato mixture from the oven and set aside.

3. Reduce the oven temperature to 400°F. Put the tomatoes in the baking dish with any accumulated juices and the roasted basil leaves. Sprinkle the Parmesan, mozzarella, and torn basil over the tomatoes. Sprinkle with the remaining 1 tablespoon olive oil. Grind pepper lightly over the tomatoes. Arrange the olives evenly over the filling. Set aside to cool while you roll the crust.

A Step Ahead: The tomatoes can be roasted a day ahead, covered, and refrigerated overnight.

Crust Options: Surefire Cream Cheese Crust (page 21) or Extremely Flaky Sour Cream Crust (page 22) can be used for this potpie. Or, use a store-bought refrigerated pie crust.

4. Lightly flour the rolling surface and rolling pin. Roll the crust dough to a shape that is about $1^1/_2$ inches larger than the top of the baking dish. Roll the crust around the rolling pin and unroll it over the top of the baking dish. Fold $3/_4$ inch of the edge of the crust under to form a smooth edge. Use your thumb and forefinger to pinch the edge into a fluted or scalloped pattern around the edge of the dish while pressing it firmly onto the rim. Use a pastry brush to brush the top of the dough lightly with the egg wash. Cut a small $1/_2$-inch hole in the center of the crust and four 2-inch-long slits in the top of the crust to release steam while the potpie bakes.

5. Bake for about 45 minutes, or until the crust edges are lightly browned and the filling begins to bubble. Let rest for 5 minutes, then use a large spoon to cut down through the crust and scoop out servings of crust and filling. Or, serve at room temperature.

ONION SHORTCAKE POTPIE

Makes **6** servings

COOKING THE FILLING:
35 MINUTES

POTPIE BAKING:
400°F FOR ABOUT
17 MINUTES

Filling

2 tablespoons unsalted butter

1 1/2 pounds onions (3 large), thinly sliced

1 teaspoon sugar

2 cloves garlic, finely chopped

2 tablespoons water

Salt and freshly ground black pepper

Topping

1 cup unbleached all-purpose flour

2 tablespoons sugar

1/2 teaspoon baking powder

1/2 teaspoon baking soda

1/4 teaspoon salt

4 tablespoons cold unsalted butter, cut into small pieces

1 cup (4 ounces) shredded sharp Cheddar cheese

1/2 cup buttermilk (nonfat is fine)

A Step Ahead: The filling can be prepared up to a day ahead, covered, and refrigerated. Make the topping when you are ready to bake the potpie.

Slow cooking meets fast baking in this dish of caramelized onions baked under a crisp Cheddar cheese biscuit crust. Cooking the onions slowly in a bit of butter brings out their natural sugar and produces the desired deep golden "caramel" color and flavor.

1. Position a rack in the middle of the oven. Preheat the oven to 400°F. Have ready a 9-inch glass pie dish or 9-inch round shallow baking dish.

2. **Make the filling:** In a large skillet, melt the butter over medium-low heat for 1 minute. Add the onions, sugar, and garlic and cook, stirring often, until the onions are soft and evenly dark golden, about 35 minutes. They will shrink in volume by about half. Pour in the water, stirring with a wooden spoon to scrape up any browned bits. Continue cooking for a few minutes until the water evaporates. The onions will turn slightly darker as they incorporate the brown bits. Remove the pan from the heat. Season with salt and pepper. Scrape the onions into the baking dish.

3. **Prepare the topping:** In a large bowl, stir the flour, sugar, baking powder, baking soda, and salt together. Add the butter pieces. Using the paddle attachment of an electric mixer on low speed, a pastry blender, or your fingertips, mix the ingredients together until coarse crumbs form, about 1/2 to 3/4 inch in size. Stir in the shredded cheese. Add the buttermilk and continue stirring just until a soft dough forms. Gather the dough into a ball. Lightly flour the rolling surface and rolling pin and roll the dough into a 9-inch circle (about 3/4 inch thick) that fits snugly into the baking dish. Use a metal spatula to loosen the dough from the rolling surface and place it over the onion filling. If the dough breaks during the transfer, just pinch it together. This dough just rests on top of the filling.

4. Bake until the top is evenly golden, about 17 minutes. Use a large knife to cut the hot pie into wedges and a wide spatula or pancake turner to lift the filling and its topping from the baking dish.

MUSHROOM RAGOUT POTPIE

1¼ pounds mushrooms,
such as portobello, cremini, shiitakes,
oysters, and/or buttons

3 tablespoons unsalted butter

2 shallots, finely chopped

4 cloves garlic, finely chopped

1 cup dry red wine

2 tablespoons fresh parsley, finely
chopped

Salt and freshly ground black pepper

Surefire Cream Cheese Crust (page 21)

Not so long ago, mushroom choice was usually limited to white button mushrooms. Now supermarkets display a veritable feast of fresh mushrooms. There are portobellos, cremini, shiitakes, oysters, and even the occasional morel. Each variety will add another texture and flavor, from subtle to assertive. For this filling, pick a variety of the freshest mushrooms, let them soak up the flavors of butter, garlic, and red wine, and enjoy the feast.

———∿∿∿∿∿∿———

1. Position a rack in the middle of the oven. Preheat the oven to 400°F. Have ready a baking dish with a 6-cup capacity.

2. Clean the mushrooms by rinsing them quickly if they have a lot of dirt clinging to them and then patting them dry with paper towels. Or, if they seem fairly clean, just wipe them with a damp paper towel. Trim the bottoms of the stems; remove and discard the stems of shiitake mushrooms, if using. They are tough. Leave any mushrooms that are about 1 inch in size whole and cut the larger ones in half or into 1-inch pieces. Slice portobellos into ¹/₂-inch-thick slices.

3. In a large skillet, melt 2 tablespoons of the butter over medium heat for 1 minute. Add the shallots and cook for about 2 minutes to soften them slightly. Stir in the garlic and mushrooms and cook until the mushrooms soften and the moisture evaporates, about 8 minutes, stirring often. The mushrooms will shrink considerably. Pour in the red wine and cook at a gentle boil, adjusting the heat if necessary, until the wine is reduced by half and the sauce turns a rich brown color, about 5 minutes. Stir in the parsley and swirl in the remaining 1 tablespoon butter. Remove the pan from the heat and season with salt and pepper. Transfer the mixture to the baking dish and let it cool for about 15 minutes while you roll the crust.

4. Lightly flour the rolling surface and rolling pin. Roll the crust dough to a shape that is 1 inch larger than the top of the baking dish. Roll the crust around the rolling pin and unroll it over the cooled mushroom filling. Fold $1/2$ inch of the edge of the crust under to form a smooth edge. Use the tines of a fork to press the dough firmly onto the rim of the baking dish. Cut four 2-inch-long slits in the top of the crust to release steam while the pie bakes.

5. Bake for about 20 minutes, or until the crust is lightly browned and the filling just begins to bubble gently. Serve the potpie by using a large spoon to cut down through the crust and scoop out servings of crust and filling.

HEARTY HUNGARIAN VEGETABLE SOUP POTPIE

1 tablespoon vegetable oil

3 cups coarsely chopped onions (3 medium)

4 carrots, peeled and sliced about 1/4 inch thick

4 large stalks celery, coarsely chopped (1 cup)

1 medium potato (8 ounces), peeled and cut into 1/2-inch pieces

1 medium red bell pepper, seeded, deveined, and coarsely chopped

4 cloves garlic, finely chopped

2 tablespoons sweet Hungarian paprika

5 cups chicken broth (low sodium if canned)

2 teaspoons fresh thyme leaves, or 1 teaspoon dried thyme

1 bay leaf

2 ounces medium-width dried egg noodles

Salt and freshly ground black pepper

1 tablespoon fresh parsley, finely chopped

You-Can-Do-It Flaky Crust (page 19)

When I was testing this recipe, we were in the midst of a nor'easter, a really big storm. We sat down to bowls of this spicy vegetable soup, thick with noodles and topped with a flaky crust that keeps it steaming hot down to the last spoonful. It is the perfect way to weather any storm.

It is fine to alter the vegetable quantities and types to suit your taste, but be sure to use sweet Hungarian paprika, which gives this soup its characteristic flavor. A nice thing happens to the crust on this soup. The crust is quite crisp on top, but the hot soup makes it soft and dumpling-like underneath.

———~~~~~~~~~———

1. Put 4 ovenproof baking dishes or ovenproof bowls with a 2-cup capacity on a baking sheet. The baking sheet makes it easier to move the baking dishes in and out of the oven.

2. In a large saucepan, heat the oil over medium-low heat. Add the onions and cook them, stirring often, until softened, about 5 minutes. Add the carrots, celery, and potato and cook until softened slightly, about 5 more minutes. Reduce the heat to low and add the bell pepper, garlic, and paprika and cook for 2 or 3 minutes, stirring constantly, until you smell the paprika. Immediately add the chicken broth, thyme, and bay leaf. Cover loosely and adjust the heat to cook the soup at a gentle simmer, stirring occasionally, until the vegetables are soft, about 35 minutes. Add the noodles and season with salt and pepper. Cook for about 10 more minutes, or until the noodles are tender. Add the parsley. Discard the bay leaf.

3. Ladle about 1 1/2 cups of soup into each baking dish. There should be at least 1/2 inch of space between the soup and the rim of the baking dish. Set aside to cool for at least 15 minutes while you roll the crust.

4. Position a rack in the middle of the oven. Preheat the oven to 375°F.

5. Cut the crust dough into 4 equal pieces, one for each bowl of soup. Lightly flour the rolling surface and rolling pin. Roll one piece of dough to a shape that is $3/4$ inch larger than the top of the baking dish. Roll the crust around the rolling pin and unroll it over the filling. Fold $1/2$ inch of the edge of the crust under itself to form a smooth edge. Use the tines of a fork to press the dough firmly onto the edge of the dish. Hold the fork at an angle to the edge to produce a nice pattern. Cut two 2-inch-long slits in the top of the crust to release steam while the potpie bakes. Repeat with the remaining 3 bowls of soup.

6. Bake for about 35 minutes, or until the crust is lightly browned and the filling is just beginning to bubble gently. The filling should not bubble vigorously, as this will make it bubble up through the crust. Protect your hands with pot holders and put the hot baking dishes on individual plates and serve.

LEEKS IN MUSTARD CREAM POTPIE

8 leeks

1 cup heavy whipping cream

2 tablespoons Dijon mustard

Salt and freshly ground black pepper

Surefire Cream Cheese Crust
(page 21)

So simple, so easy, and yet so sophisticated. This dish reminds me of something you would be served in France, at the home of a very good cook. The leeks take on the rich flavor of mustard and cream as they bake.

NOTE: Leeks often have sand caught between their layers and should be cleaned by halving them lengthwise and washing them thoroughly.

~~~~~~~~~~~~~~

1. Position a rack in the middle of the oven. Preheat the oven to 375°F. Have ready a 9-by-2-inch round or oval baking dish or glass pie dish.

2. Cut off the green part of the leeks and discard or use for soup. Cut the white part in half lengthwise. Rinse thoroughly to wash away any sand between the layers and cut the leeks into 1-inch pieces. You will have about 4 cups. In a medium bowl, stir the cream and mustard together. Add the leek pieces, and season with salt and pepper. Use a rubber spatula to stir the mixture together and coat the leeks with liquid. Use the spatula to scrape all of the leek filling into the baking dish. Set aside.

3. Lightly flour the rolling surface and rolling pin. Roll the crust dough to a shape that is 1 inch larger than the top of the baking dish. Roll the dough around the rolling pin and unroll it over the leek filling. Fold 1/2 inch of the edge of the dough under to form a smooth edge. Use a fork to press the dough firmly onto the rim of the baking dish. Cut four 2-inch-long slits in the top of the crust to release steam while the potpie bakes.

4. Bake for about 40 minutes, or until the crust is lightly browned and the filling is bubbling gently. Use a large spoon to cut down through the crust and scoop out servings of crust and filling.

A Step Ahead: The potpie can be assembled early in the day, covered, and refrigerated, then baked when you need it. A cold potpie will need about 5 additional minutes of baking time.

Crust Options: You-Can-Do-It Flaky Crust (page 19) or Extremely Flaky Sour Cream Crust (page 22) can be used for this potpie. Or, use a store-bought refrigerated pie crust.

ONION, SPRING ONION & POTATO POTPIE

Filling

2 tablespoons unsalted butter

4 cups coarsely chopped onions (4 medium)

2 cups finely chopped green onions (about 12), including green parts

2 pounds potatoes (about 4 medium), peeled and cut into 1/2- to 2-inch pieces

3/4 teaspoon salt

3 large eggs, lightly beaten

1/2 teaspoon freshly ground black pepper

Topping

4 phyllo pastry sheets (about 13 by 17 inches), thawed if frozen

1 tablespoon unsalted butter, melted

Pile on the onions. It is the half-onion, half-potato combination that makes such a well-seasoned filling for this potpie. Store-bought phyllo pastry makes an instant crisp, light topping. Since this potpie is good served hot or at room temperature and has a no-spill filling, it is a good choice for a picnic or potluck.

———————~~~~~~~~~———————

1. Position a rack in the middle of the oven. Preheat the oven to 375°F. Have ready a 9-by-2-inch round baking dish or glass pie dish.

2. Make the filling: In a large skillet, melt the butter over medium heat. Add the onions and green onions and cook until the onions soften and brown lightly, about 17 minutes, stirring often. Set aside to cool slightly.

3. While the onions cook, put the potatoes in a medium saucepan, fill it with enough water to cover the potatoes, and sprinkle in 1/4 teaspoon of the salt. Cover the pot and bring the water to a boil over high heat, then adjust the heat to cook the potatoes at a gentle simmer until they test tender with a fork, about 20 minutes. Drain the potatoes and put them in a large bowl. Use an electric mixer on low speed to mix the potatoes smoothly or a potato masher to mash them. Stir in the cooked onions, eggs, remaining 1/2 teaspoon salt, and the pepper to combine them. Spread the filling in the prepared dish.

4. Prepare the topping: Spread out the phyllo sheets in a stack. Use plastic wrap to roll up and tightly rewrap any leftover phyllo and refrigerate it for up to 1 week. Using the bottom of the baking dish as a guide, use kitchen scissors to cut 4 pieces of phyllo that are 2 inches larger all around than the baking dish. Keep the cut sheets of phyllo covered with a damp dish towel.

5. Place 2 pieces of the phyllo pastry on top of the filling in the dish. Brush the pastry lightly with melted butter. Top with the remaining 2 pieces of phyllo and brush with the remaining butter. Tuck any overhanging edges underneath to form a smooth edge that neatly covers the filling. Use a sharp knife to mark 10 wedges by cutting through the top layers of pastry.

6. Bake until the phyllo topping is golden, about 35 minutes. Use a sharp knife to cut through the marked wedges and a spatula with a wide blade to remove the wedges and serve.

BLACK BEAN CHILI POTPIE WITH ONION & PEPPER CORN BREAD TOPPING

Filling

1¼ cups (½ pound) dried black beans

1 bay leaf

1½ teaspoons dried oregano

2 teaspoons chili powder, plus 1 tablespoon

½ teaspoon ground cumin

1 ancho chile, dried

One 14½-ounce can tomatoes

2 tablespoons olive oil

3 cups coarsely chopped onions

1 large green bell pepper, seeded, deveined, and finely chopped

3 cloves garlic, finely chopped

Salt and freshly ground black pepper

Topping

½ cup unbleached all-purpose flour

⅔ cup yellow cornmeal

2 tablespoons sugar

1 teaspoon baking powder

½ teaspoon baking soda

¼ teaspoon salt

⅔ cup buttermilk

1 large egg

1 tablespoon corn oil

Reserved ½ cup cooked vegetables from filling, above

Black beans and tomatoes form the base for this rich vegetarian chili filling. The batter for the topping is seasoned with some of the vegetables and bakes into a crisp, firm topping. Cooking an ancho chile (a dried poblano) with the beans adds a great deal to the rich flavor. Ancho chiles can be ordered from Penzeys (see Sources, page 130). Taste chili powder to make sure that it is fresh, because over-the-hill chili powder will have no flavor at all. Although cooking the beans takes a bit of time, they really only need an occasional glance and a quick stir.

———~~~~~~~~———

1. Make the filling: Wash the beans in a strainer and check for any debris or small pebbles. Put the beans in a large bowl, cover them with water, and let them soak overnight. Or, put the beans in a medium saucepan, cover them with water, and bring it to boil. Turn off the heat and let the beans sit for 1 hour. Drain the beans. Put the soaked beans in a large saucepan with water to cover them by about 2 inches. Add the bay leaf, 1 teaspoon of the oregano, the 2 teaspoons chili powder, the cumin, and ancho chile. Cover and cook for 30 minutes. Add the tomatoes with their juice and cook about 45 more minutes, or until the beans are tender. Taste a bean to check that they are done.

2. Have ready a baking dish with an 8-cup capacity. In a medium skillet, heat the oil over medium heat for 1 minute. Add the onions and cook until softened, stirring often, about 5 minutes. Add the bell pepper and garlic and continue cooking until the pepper is soft, about 8 minutes. Remove ½ cup of the vegetables and reserve them to add to the topping later. Stir the remaining 1 tablespoon chili powder and ½ teaspoon oregano into the vegetables in the skillet.

Continued

Stir the vegetables into the beans. Remove the ancho chile and bay leaf and discard them. Remove 1 cup of the beans, put it in a food processor, and purée. Return the purée to the beans and stir them together. This thickens the chili. Season with salt and pepper. Pour the chili into the baking dish and set aside.

3. Position an oven rack in the middle of the oven. Preheat the oven to 375°F.

4. Prepare the topping: Into a large bowl, sift the flour, cornmeal, sugar, baking powder, baking soda, and salt. In a medium bowl, stir the buttermilk, egg, oil, and reserved cooked vegetables together to combine them. Pour the buttermilk mixture into the dry ingredients and stir slowly with a large spoon for about 20 strokes just to combine the ingredients. There will be a few small lumps. This is fine. Carefully spoon the batter over the chili in the baking dish.

5. Bake until the topping is golden brown and firm, about 35 minutes. Use a large spoon to scoop out servings of topping and filling.

SPINACH, RICOTTA & PARMESAN POTPIE

1 tablespoon unsalted butter

1 cup coarsely chopped onion
(1 medium)

1 pound baby spinach leaves
or regular spinach, stemmed

2 large eggs, lightly beaten

1 cup ricotta cheese (part skim is fine)

1 cup (4 ounces) freshly grated
Parmesan cheese

1/2 teaspoon salt

1/4 teaspoon freshly ground
black pepper

Surefire Cream Cheese Crust (page 21)

This was a huge hit when I brought it as my contribution to a potluck dinner. I baked it before I left home and served it room temperature, but it is also good hot out of the oven. This potpie uses fresh spinach and has a light-textured filling. One pound of fresh spinach has a lot of bulk, but it shrinks considerably when it cooks.

———∿∿∿∿∿∿———

1. Position a rack in the middle of the oven. Preheat the oven to 375°F. Have ready a 6-cup capacity baking dish.

2. In a large saucepan that has at least a 5-quart capacity, melt the butter over medium heat for about 1 minute. Add the onion and cook until it softens, about 5 minutes, stirring often. Rinse the spinach and add it to the saucepan along with any water that clings to the leaves. Cover and cook until the spinach shrinks and darkens in color, about 5 minutes. Uncover the pan and continue cooking until all of the moisture has evaporated, about 5 minutes. Transfer the spinach mixture to a plate to cool slightly. Drain off any liquid that accumulates. As soon as the spinach is cool enough to handle, squeeze it dry and use a large knife to chop it coarsely.

3. In a large bowl, stir the eggs, ricotta, and Parmesan cheese together to combine them. Add the spinach, salt, and pepper and stir to blend the spinach evenly into the filling. Use a rubber spatula to scrape all of the filling into the baking dish.

Continued

4. Lightly flour the rolling surface and rolling pin. Roll the crust dough to a shape that is 2 inches larger than the top of the baking dish. Roll the dough around the rolling pin and unroll it over the spinach filling. Fold $1/2$ inch of the edge of the dough under to form a smooth edge, then roll the edges to make a rope of crust, or use the tines of a fork to press the dough firmly onto the rim of the baking dish.

5. Bake for about 40 minutes, or until the crust is lightly browned and the filling is sizzling gently. Use a large spoon to cut down through the crust and scoop out servings of crust and filling.

ZUCCHINI POTPIE WITH A CHEDDAR WAFER CRUST

Makes 8

COOKING THE FILLING:
21 MINUTES

POTPIE BAKING:
350°F FOR ABOUT
45 MINUTES

Filling

2 pounds small young zucchini
(about 10)

3 tablespoons unsalted butter

1¼ cups finely chopped onion
(1 medium-large)

2 cloves garlic, finely chopped

½ teaspoon salt

¼ teaspoon freshly ground
black pepper

2 large eggs, lightly beaten

Topping

1 cup (4 ounces) shredded
sharp Cheddar cheese

½ cup (1 stick) unsalted butter
at room temperature

1 cup unbleached all-purpose flour

¼ teaspoon salt

½ teaspoon garlic powder

½ teaspoon mustard powder

1 teaspoon Worcestershire sauce

In summer, zucchini rule. It is amazing what a few spring-planted seeds can produce. My "zucchini defense" is to enjoy the bounty and let them dominate, as in this potpie. Another idea for keeping the crop under control is to pick zucchini when they are young and at their best. These smaller zucchini have few seeds and less water, and that adds up to more flavor. Cheddar wafers (actually a savory cookie) make the pretty scalloped pattern for the topping.

~~~~~~~~~~~~~~~~

1. Position an oven rack in the middle of the oven. Preheat the oven to 350°F. Have ready a baking dish with a 6-cup capacity.

2. Make the filling: Use a vegetable brush to scrub the zucchini and rid the peel of any sand. Trim off the ends and cut each zucchini lengthwise into strips about ¼ inch thick (about 6 strips). Hold a few strips together and cut them into thin slices ⅛ to ¼ inch thick. Set aside. This is a quick way to chop the zucchini into small pieces.

3. In a large skillet, melt 1 tablespoon of the butter over medium-high heat for 1 minute. Add the onion and garlic and cook just until the onion softens, about 5 minutes, stirring often. Transfer the onion mixture to a large bowl. Melt the remaining 2 tablespoons butter in the pan over medium heat. Add the zucchini and cook, stirring often, until most of the moisture evaporates and the zucchini soften, about 15 minutes. Transfer the zucchini to the large bowl. Add the salt and pepper. Stir in the eggs to blend them into the mixture. Transfer the mixture to the baking dish.

4. Prepare the topping: In a large bowl and using an electric mixer on low speed, beat the cheese and butter until smoothly blended. You will see small pieces of cheese. Beat in the flour, salt, garlic powder, mustard powder, and Worcestershire until a smooth dough forms that holds together. Use your hands to roll level tablespoon-sized pieces of dough into balls about $1^{1}/_{4}$ inches in size. Flatten them into round wafers. You will have 24 wafers. Place a circle of overlapping wafers on the zucchini filling around the inside edge of the baking dish. Place another circle inside the outer circle and 1 wafer in the center. The wafers will cover the filling. If there are a few tiny uncovered spaces, these will fill in as the potpie bakes.

5. Bake until the topping is lightly browned and feels firm when lightly touched, about 45 minutes. Use a large spoon to cut down through the crust and scoop out servings of crust and filling.

SOURCES

Bridge Kitchenware
711 Third Avenue (45th Street)
New York, NY 10017
(800) 274-3435; Fax: (212) 758-5387
www.bridgekitchenware.com
A large selection of saucepans, skillets, utensils, knives, parchment paper, and baking containers.

King Arthur Flour Baker's Catalogue
P. O. Box 876
Norwich, VT 05055
(800) 827-6836; Fax: (800) 343-3002
www.kingarthurflour.com
A selection of equipment, baking pans, and containers.

Morse's Sauerkraut
Route 220
Waldoboro, ME 04572
(207) 832-5569; Fax: (207) 832-2297
www.morsessauerkraut.com
Fresh sauerkraut and a large variety of sausages.

Penzeys Spices
P. O. Box 924
19300 West Janacek Court
Brookfield, WI 53008
(800) 741-7787; Fax: (262) 785-7678
www.penzeys.com
A complete selection of herbs and spices.

Williams-Sonoma
P.O. Box 379900
Las Vegas, NV 89137
(800) 541-2233; Fax: (702) 363-2541
www.williams-sonoma.com
A large selection of equipment, ingredients, and baking containers.

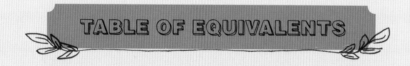

TABLE OF EQUIVALENTS

The exact equivalents in the following tables have been rounded for convenience.

LIQUID/DRY MEASURES

U.S.		Metric	
¼	teaspoon	1.25	milliliters
½	teaspoon	2.5	milliliters
1	teaspoon	5	milliliters
1	tablespoon (3 teaspoons)	15	milliliters
1	fluid ounce (2 tablespoons)	30	milliliters
¼	cup	60	milliliters
⅓	cup	80	milliliters
½	cup	120	milliliters
1	cup	240	milliliters
1	pint (2 cups)	480	milliliters
1	quart (4 cups, 32 ounces)	960	milliliters
1	gallon (4 quarts)	3.84	liters
1	ounce (by weight)	28	grams
1	pound	454	grams
2.2	pounds	1	kilogram

LENGTHS

U.S.	Metric	
⅛ inch	3	millimeters
¼ inch	6	millimeters
½ inch	12	millimeters
1 inch	2.5	centimeters

OVEN TEMPERATURES

Fahrenheit	Celsius	Gas
250	120	½
275	140	1
300	150	2
325	160	3
350	180	4
375	190	5
400	200	6
425	220	7
450	230	8
475	240	9
500	260	10

INDEX

INDEX